Look Up!

Look Up!

Birds and Other Natural Wonders
Just Outside Your Window

To Beth & Marsha,

Keep looking up!

Woody Wheeler

First Published in Canada 2014 by Influence Publishing

Cover design and layout: Marla Thompson
Cover photo of Golden-crowned Kinglet: Jeff Larsen
Author photo: Larry Hubbell
Typesetting: Greg Salisbury

DISCLAIMER: This book is a work of Non-Fiction. Some of the names of characters in this book may have been changed to protect their anonymity.

Library and Archives Canada Cataloguing in Publication

Wheeler, Woody, 1951-, author
        Look up! / Woody Wheeler.

Includes bibliographical references.
ISBN 978-1-77141-062-5 (pbk.)

        1. Human ecology. 2. Wheeler, Woody, 1951- --Anecdotes.
I. Title.

GF47.W44 2014   304.2   C2014-904460-7

To my great grandfather, Jens Jensen, whose conservation legacy continues to inspire me, and to my daughters, Leah and Audrey, who strive for a positive, sustainable future.

Testimonials

"Of the many writers who have trained their focus on birds and their encompassing world, few have covered so much territory in so little space as Woody Wheeler. In these compact and companionable essays, "Look Up!" finds the essential fascination in subjects ranging from sapsuckers and nutcrackers to waxwings and zombies, Loraxes and Roosevelts to pikas and bikes. Besides spotting the birds, often by bike, Woody also takes on the bugaboos of our disconnected age, whether hand-helds, leaf-blowers, or science-deniers—and suggests how we may easily connect anew, just by "Looking Up!" This is a book that celebrates the full range of what we are given, from the lowly dump and tiny wren, to the resplendent quetzal and scarlet macaw. I very much doubt you will take it to bed and not face the next morning with an entirely new appreciation for birds, and for the quirky world we are lucky enough to occupy together."
Robert Michael Pyle, Author of Wintergreen, Mariposa Road, and The Tangled Bank

"Woody offers a fresh perspective, freely sharing knowledge of ecology, bird behavior and the critical component of conservation."
Peg Abbott, Executive Director, Naturalist Journeys

"Woody always does such a great job of introducing people to birding and inspiring them to make it a part of their lives."
Jeff Parsons, Founding Director, Barn Beach Reserve – Leavenworth, WA

Acknowledgements

First and foremost I thank my wife, Lori, who shares my passion for conservation and has supported me throughout my career, including during this recent chapter as a new author. Her tireless, capable editing for the past five years significantly shaped and refined this book.

To Jeff Larsen, fabulous bird and nature photographer, I owe great thanks for providing spectacular photos that grace this book and my website. Visit his website to see truly inspiring photos of birds and wildlife in action: www.jefflarsen.com

Hilary Hilscher and Neil Johannsen, great conservationists and friends, deserve special thanks for encouraging me to follow this path of nature interpretation, teaching and writing.

Thank you to neighbor and web engineer extraordinaire Jigna Patel for suggesting five years ago that I write blogs to activate my then new business website. These blogs morphed into the essays that fill this book.

To Jeff Parsons, thank you for planting a seed of an idea when you suggested that I return to the Barn Beach Reserve Center in Leavenworth with a book that I have written some day. Here it is, Jeff!

Jan Vallone, author, teacher, and neighbor, who urged me to write this book and provided important perspective on the brave new world (for me) of writing and publishing books.

To Peg Abbott and Naturalist Journeys, I thank you for hiring me to guide such memorable journeys in North and Central America. These journeys inspired quite a few of these essays. To anyone interested in going on them, please visit their website: www.naturalist-journeys.com

To Celise Spencer and the Cedar River Watershed Center, I owe thanks for helping me make the transition to this path of leading birding and natural history tours by hiring me to teach Family-friendly Birding classes six years ago.

To Larry Pennings, career coach, I owe you major thanks for strongly recommending that I teach the class at the Cedar River Watershed Center as a first step toward a much-desired career shift. It was a pivotal change; small steps do lead to bigger ones.

Thanks to Elaine Harvey, whose Facebook "like" encouraged me to investigate Influence Publishing.

Many thanks to those who provided photographs to enhance this book, including: John Carlson, my wife Lori Cohen, Kyle and Melanie Elliot, Larry Hubbell, Jeff Larsen, Christopher Moffett, Teri Pieper, Heather Phillips, and Gregg Thompson.

To everyone else who provided encouragement and guidance along the way, I offer my sincere thanks. I also wish to apologize in advance to anyone I inadvertently omitted.

Contents

Chapter 1 - Getting to Know Your Avian Neighbors

Green Heron
©Woody Wheeler

Blame the Waxwings

Long ago, a Midwestern boy was trained to be a crossing guard at Harper Elementary School in Wilmette, Illinois. Perhaps due to his shyness, or his small stature, he was assigned to the farthest, most remote crossing from the school. What it lacked in car traffic it made up for in bird traffic. The crossing was in a peaceful area overhung by a row of crabapple trees. One fall morning during a lull in crossing activity, he noticed colorful birds flitting through one of the crabapple trees. Looking more closely, he saw a dozen gorgeous yellow and brown birds with crested heads and brilliant red and yellow accents feeding on the crabapples. The birds seemed tame.

Early the next morning, he rode his bike to his crossing and found several trees swarming with even more of these birds. He got to within ten feet of them as they feasted on the crabapples. He stood transfixed for an hour, a witness to a miraculous event.

Back at home, the boy searched through the family bird book and found the birds he had been observing. They were Cedar Waxwings. There was something intoxicating about all of this. Later in life, he discovered that because the birds had been eating overripe crabapples they were indeed intoxicated. This made them tame and approachable.

This boy has been watching and studying birds ever since. As you might have guessed by now, this boy was me. The essays that follow derive from this formative experience and from many more similar experiences I've had since. It is my sincere hope that readers of this book will take the time to go outdoors more often and look up to find the wonder and inspiration that awaits them.

Cedar Waxwing

Back Row Birder

Remember when K-12 schools seated students in alphabetic order? Have you ever wondered what effects these charts had on us—especially for those of us whose last names were at the end of the alphabet?

Recently, a marketing study conducted by researchers from Georgetown and Belmont Universities addressed this issue from a standpoint of its impact on purchasing behavior. The study suggests that people whose surnames are toward the end of the alphabet purchase products more quickly, and that this behavior is attributable to their position as last in line throughout their K-12 schooling days. Since my initials are WW, I was seated in the back corner of every classroom in the Illinois K-12 schools I attended. Ironically, this positioning also fostered my interest in birding. How? Because I almost always sat next to the window where I could watch the birds in the trees outside. The action in the trees was closer in proximity than the action at the front of the class. Just for the record, I do make purchasing decisions quickly.

Pileated Woodpecker
© Woody Wheeler

Woody Woodpecker Revisited

Sometimes I wish all memory of this old, unremarkable cartoon would vanish, but it persists. Ever since grade school, when people meet me, they often pause for a moment as if they were the first creative genius to come up with it, chuckle and say, "You mean like Woody Woodpecker?" It's even worse when they find out that I am a birding and natural history tour guide.

Oh, well! There's no hiding from this association with a bad cartoon. It turns out that woodpeckers and I do have several things in common: we like mature forests, we play the drums (I did in my younger days), and we have hard heads (just ask my sisters or my wife). Let's take a brief look at why these three associations are important to woodpeckers.

Mature Forests

Woodpeckers like the Pileated Woodpecker pictured on the previous page are especially fond of mature forests. According to the *Bird Biology Handbook* of the Cornell Lab of Ornithology, one Pileated Woodpecker requires at least 250 acres of forest. Roughly the size of a crow, these large woodpeckers depend upon large trees with rotting wood and standing snags to find their food, which consists primarily of carpenter ants and wood-boring beetles buried in the rotting bark. They reside in tree cavities, often in dead trees, so they need the older forest not only for food, but also for shelter.

Drumming

Woodpeckers play the drums, so to speak, because they cannot sing in the spring breeding season. Drumming is how woodpeckers communicate with potential mates and defend their territory. Often the drumming happens on trees, but sometimes, especially with Northern Flickers, it happens on your stovepipe or chimney. They like the resonant sound, which may be off-putting to you when it occurs at 5:00 a.m.

Hard Heads

Why the hard heads? It should be obvious. Woodpeckers need a hard head to withstand the frequent pounding as they excavate holes for food and shelter, and when they drum. Actually, their skulls are not only hard and thick, they are also filled with spongy material and fluid to protect the brain. Woodpecker skulls have been studied in order to design various helmets that protect human heads.

It turns out that woodpeckers and I have far more in common in real life than I do with the obnoxious character in the cartoon. In the end, I embrace my association with that high-profile woodpecker.

Go East, Young Finch!

As I write this, I am being serenaded by the bubbly song of a House Finch just outside my window. House Finches are prolific singers. These cheerful, colorful birds that frequent our yards and feeders have an interesting story.

Native to North America and Mexico, House Finches are typically found not only at feeders, residential yards, and city parks, but also where they came from: deserts, grasslands, the chaparral, and open forests. House Finches are superabundant. According to the Cornell Lab of Ornithology, there are now at least 267 million House Finches distributed throughout most of North America and Mexico, except for a band of territory without finches that runs through the Great Plains States. Although relatively small in stature, House Finches have sizeable beaks that enable them to eat their favorite foods: seeds, buds, and fruits.

They were not always found in the Eastern parts of North America. We often hear the story of birds like the European Starling and House Sparrow that were introduced from Europe to the Eastern U.S. and later spread west. House Finches, on the other hand, were introduced from the Western to the Eastern U.S.

The Cornell Lab of Ornithology *Bird Biology Handbook* chronicles this event: "In the early 1940s … House Finches from a sedentary population in California were released on Long Island, New York. The introduction was wildly successful, and House Finches have become one of the most abundant birds in urban and suburban areas of the northeastern United States." According to *Partners in Flight*, the majority of the House Finch population now breeds in the U.S. (76 percent). Mexico has the next largest breeding population at 21 percent, followed by Canada at 3 percent. Now this colorful, sociable bird with the cheerful song is a frequent companion to many of us. The two House Finches watching me from our feeder as I write verify this. There might be a few in your backyard right now.

Avian Architects

Bushtit Nest
© Woody Wheeler

Have you ever marveled at the sight of Bushtits squeezing in and out of a perfectly sized hole in one of their hanging thatched nests? It's one of the miracles that you can witness in the western part of North America if you keep your eyes and ears open and your head up. These very small (4.5 inches long), cute gray birds with long tails build intricate nests. Picture these tiny birds weaving foot-long pendulous nests made of spider webs and plant material with their tiny bills and feet. They manage to assemble these durable, camouflaged structures within a two-month timeframe. Then they move in with their mate to raise their families until the young fledge. At that point, they move out and sleep on branches.

Imagine making a nest like this. Let's say that you even received detailed instructions on how to build it. Using your eyes and the great dexterity of human hands, you do your best to carefully weave it, install it on a tree, and hope it will last. Would it be able to withstand windstorms, would it hold up to the Bushtit family coming and going, and would it be effectively camouflaged? I don't think so.

The sociable and vocal Bushtits, with their soft, high-pitched, repetitive call, are thankfully not a species at risk. You will find them in groups of up to forty searching for spiders and bugs, sometimes upside down, in the western/southwestern U.S. and Mexico. Just watch a shrub near you to find them. Or they might pay a visit to your feeder. You will only notice them, however, if you look up.

Carbo-Loading for Migration

Black-headed Grosbeak
© Woody Wheeler

If you have bird feeders, have you ever noticed how certain birds camp out on your feeder for extended periods of time? If this happens in the fall, they might just be carbo-loading for migration.

One fall, a loud "chink" call announced the presence of these stocky, colorful, and (as the name implies) large-beaked birds to our backyard. A pair of chunky Black-headed Grosbeaks was camped out on our feeder. Common in the Western and Central North America during their summer breeding season, these birds were fueling up for their fall migration to Baja and Western Mexico.

During their previous spring migration, Black-headed Grosbeaks arrived in my backyard in May. In the spring they are prolific singers with a florid, whistled tune that birders say sounds like a drunken robin. Unlike most songbirds, both male and female Black-headed Grosbeaks sing. The showboat male with its bright orange and black plumage and its impressive vocal talents also shares home-making duties with the female: sitting on the eggs, feeding the young, and defending the territory. Fortunately, the buoyant song of the Black-headed Grosbeak shouldn't fade from western forests, wetlands, and backyards. According to the Cornell Lab of Ornithology, the Black-headed Grosbeak is not a declining species. In fact its numbers might actually be increasing.

The pair in our yard was so heavy that they sometimes tipped the feeder. They stayed for an entire week, rarely abandoning the feeder. I wished them well on their flight to Mexico and hope to see and hear them once again in the spring.

Anna's World

Anna's Hummingbird
© Woody Wheeler

If you have been on the West Coast of North America lately, you might have seen Anna's Hummingbirds. This species seems to be adapting well to the human-altered landscape. Nationally renowned birder/author Kenn Kaufman refers to Anna's as "the familiar year-round hummer of the west coast...."

Anna's Hummingbirds have dramatically expanded their original range in Baja California and western California to include the entire Pacific Coast, extending north to British Columbia and east to Arizona and Texas. Why the range expansion in this era of degraded and often declining habitat for many species? Anna's Hummingbirds benefit from cultivated, exotic plants that bloom all year long, and from the widespread use of sugar-water feeders. Climate change might be a factor too.

Another interesting aspect of the range expansion is that Anna's have become year-round residents in the northern reaches of the range, such as the Seattle area. How does this tiny bird survive cold winters? Anna's and other hummingbirds are capable of going into a state of torpor. In this state, they lower their metabolism significantly during periods of cold temperatures, especially at night.

Named after Anna de Rivoli, wife of the Duke of Rivoli, an amateur French ornithologist, Anna's are showy birds that vocalize more often than most hummingbirds. You can often hear the squeaky, raspy, song of the male. If you have the good fortune to spot a male Anna's Hummingbird, its iridescent plumage flashes a spectacular bright magenta when the light hits it at just the right angle. As the weather warms and brightens, Anna's males mark their territories by flying straight up into the sky, nearly disappearing from view before dropping precipitously down and looping back up again. They make a loud "chirp" noise at the bottom of their dive. The chirp is not a vocalization; the sound is caused by their tail feathers.

Anna's nests are hard to spot and amazingly compact. They

are made of plant down and spider webs. Lichens are often used for camouflage. Hummingbirds are fiercely protective of their food and nest, and Anna's are no exception. I watched one depart from our backyard feeder to chase a Bald Eagle flying above our house. The resident Anna's seldom allows a second hummingbird to share our six-port feeder.

Having sufficient, reliable food is vital; hummingbirds can eat up to twice their body weight in nectar per day, along with numerous small insects or spiders. The many backyard feeders, seeming to multiply each year, provide lots of supplementary sugar water.

When it snows, or whenever temperatures dip below freezing at night, bring the feeder inside to thaw it out. You can bring it inside overnight and put it back out early in the morning. Anna's Hummingbirds are incredibly hungry during cold spells and sometimes will land on the feeder while you are holding it! In fact, if you don't keep the feeder filled and thawed all winter, the Anna's Hummingbirds that have been depending on it may starve.

Being a part of "Anna's World" is a great pleasure. They are worthy of their royal name. Look up to find a royal flash of color in the treetops where they perch and sing, and then search for them dipping their long bills into the tubular blossoms and the hummingbird feeders they frequent.

Bird Brainy

Clark's Nutcracker
© Teri Pieper

According to *Webster's New World Dictionary*, the expression "bird brain" is a colloquial expression for a "stupid or silly person." It is also demeaning of the intelligence of birds. Who are we to call another species stupid or silly?

Several years ago, *Newsweek* gave the U.S. Citizenship Test to one thousand Americans. Thirty-eight percent failed! Among the questions were the following: What is the name of the vice president of the United States now? What is the economic system in the United States? And what ocean is on the West Coast of the United States?

Now let's return to the expression "bird brains." Are birds really stupid? Consider Clark's Nutcracker. This handsome denizen of high mountain forests and alpine meadows of the Western U.S. and Canada was named by William Clark of the Lewis and Clark expedition. Clark's Nutcrackers gather and cache thousands of pine seeds from pine cones annually. Remarkably, they can remember where to find most of the seeds that they cache.

Another intelligent bird is the American Crow. Crows are not only smart, but they can use tools. In one experiment, a crow was placed in a closed room with food at the bottom of a narrow-necked jar. Beside the jar was a straight length of wire. Within thirty seconds, the crow, having first attempted to reach for the food with its bill, picked up the wire and used it as a tool to fish the food out of the jar.

Looking for geographic competence? Then look no further than the Arctic Tern. This bird migrates 44,000 miles every year, traveling from the Arctic to the Antarctic and back again, crossing two major oceans in the process. Although this is the longest-known migration of any bird, let alone of any animal species, many other birds travel far and use sophisticated means of navigating. Many Americans can't tell which way is north or south without the aid of GPS technology to guide us to our destinations. Birds like the Arctic Tern have their own built-in navigation system.

As a final bird intelligence note, among many bird species, the female is believed to select a mate, not vice-versa. Hearing this, my wife immediately said, "Smart birds!" Perhaps we should aspire to have bird brains. Clearly our human brains are in need of improvement, or at least stimulation and exercise. Now where did I leave my keys?

Singing Sensation

Pacific Wren
© Larry Hubbell

Sometimes the finest singers can be heard free of charge in the deep moist woods. This is certainly true of the Pacific Wren. Formerly referred to as Winter Wrens, in 2010 the species was split into Pacific Wrens along the Pacific Coast from Alaska to Northern California and east to Idaho, and Winter Wrens across central and eastern North America. Song differences between the two groups were part of the reason for the split.

Below the tall evergreen trees, along the stream banks, in and around shrubs and woody debris, you will find these wrens singing their hearts out—especially when there is a glimmer of light. These little forest dwellers feed on a combination of insects, insect larvae, millipedes, spiders, and the occasional berry.

After you hear their song, an elaborate combination of warbling trills that seems to go on forever, you feel like applauding. How can such a virtuoso singing performance come out of such a small bird?

At three to four ounces in weight and three to five inches in length, you would not think that either Winter Wrens or Pacific Wrens could produce much of a song. Prior to the split Winter Wrens had the longest song of any North American bird species. The Cornell Lab's *All About Birds* website (www.allaboutbirds.org) refers to Winter Wrens as "small in stature and incomparably energetic in voice." Per unit weight, the Winter Wren's song is ten times more powerful than a crowing rooster. Their vocalizations have been referred to as "the pinnacle of song complexity." Each song contains about forty notes and can last from ten to forty seconds. Pacific Wrens have even longer and more varied songs than do Winter Wrens.

In eastern British Columbia, the range of the two species overlaps. Every spring, an annual "battle of the wrens" sing-off takes place near the Murray River. Males of both species sing within earshot of one another. Meanwhile the female wrens listen closely. Female songbirds, including wrens, generally select their mates. Based on DNA sampling, the female Winter and Pacific Wrens select mates who sing the same song that they do. Thus, interbreeding between these two species seldom occurs.

The Winter and Pacific Wren songs are as beautiful as the forests they inhabit. They provide yet another reason to save the mature forests that still remain. Their song is not to be missed in this lifetime by anyone who appreciates music—whether performed by a human or a tiny bird.

Chapter 2 - Renewing the Spirit

Zombies Walking Amok

You've seen them in parades. You've seen them in movies. You've read about them in books and stories. They are gruesome, scary, lifeless, and at the mercy of a controlling force. Are zombies just fantasy creatures or do they actually exist? I think they are here now and their numbers are increasing.

You can see them on their way to work, on city streets, in restaurants, and coffee shops. They are the ones with their heads down, looking at the ground, or into a mobile electronic device that consumes their attention. They don't look at you or anyone else. They don't look around. They definitely do not look up; they are oblivious to their surroundings. Sometimes they seemingly talk to themselves while on earpiece phone calls. These are modern-day zombies.

The zombie connection is real. Allow me to explain. But first, here is the definition of a zombie from *Webster's New World Dictionary* : "...in West Indian superstition, a supernatural power through which a corpse supposedly is brought to a state of trance-like animation and made to obey the commands of the person exercising the power." Or as slang: "a person considered to be like a zombie in listlessness, mechanical behavior, etc."

Our pedestrian zombies have sacrificed their souls and a lot of their money to the god of technology. This is not a blood-sucking god, but a money-sucking god. And this god has its victims just where it wants them—hopelessly addicted to its product! But what about the "bloody" part? Aren't zombies the walking dead, often with gaping wounds? There is a blood connection and it is this: our modern-day zombies often get wounded or killed because they are so focused on their mobile

devices that they become dangerously unaware of their surroundings and get hit by a car, bus, truck, or train. In addition,
tens of thousands are killed each year by texting while driving.
In 2013, the number of teenage auto fatalities from texting
while driving surpassed the number of deaths due to driving
under the influence of alcohol.

Am I being overly dramatic here? Consider that in
Washington State alone, two people were struck and killed by
trains in a three-year period because they were so absorbed
by their electronic devices that they did not even notice that
the trains were approaching. According to a recent article in
the *Seattle Times*, The Consumer Product Safety Commission
reported more than 1,100 people were treated in hospitals or
emergency wards in the past year for injuries received while using a mobile electronic device while walking. We can multitask
to a degree, but the truth is we're not very good at it and we do
it at our own peril.

If we fail to pay attention to our surroundings, Charles
Darwin might have the final word. As comedian Steven Wright
is quoted in the *Darwin Awards* book, "The problem with the
gene pool is, there is no life guard."

Aside from the life-and-death consequences of zombie behavior, perhaps the greatest tragedy is that these people don't
live in the present. This means that modern zombies seldom
experience nature, the weather, sights, sounds of their environment, or the people around them. They miss a lot. They miss
life itself. They fail to look up and notice the cues, the dangers,
and the wonders all around them.

Zen Buddhists used to remind us to "Be here now." These
zombies are just the opposite: their minds and senses are somewhere else now.

As I write this, a crow has just made its third flight forty feet
up to where it dropped a chestnut onto the street below, trying
to break it open. The third time was the charm; he is now eating

the nut. Watching this was an amusing, interesting spectacle. If I had been glued to my phone, iPad, or laptop (yes I use all of these things, but sparingly), I would not have seen this. It gave me a smile. It is one of those daily sensations that help make being alive special.

A *Seattle Times* story about the dangers of distracted pedestrians offered safety tips. Number one was "Pick your head up," or as I say, "Look up. Zombies, throw off your technological shackles! Try something else extraordinary that is free. Look up and engage your senses. You might like it."

Is Faster Better?

Faster is better? Not for this guy!
Male House Sparrow © Woody Wheeler

A pervasive TV and radio ad promotes "smart" phones in a phony focus-group setting where an adult feeds corporate slogans to a group of kids. A dapper young man in a business suit and tie with an authoritative newscaster voice conducts this "focus group" with a handful of kids aged approximately eight- to ten-years-old seated around a small round table. The man then asks the kids two questions: 1) What's better? Faster or slower; and 2) What's better? Doing one thing at a time or doing several things at once? The kids respond slavishly to the messages foisted upon them with a little spontaneity around the edges. These ads reinforce two cultural mantras: 1) That faster is better than slower; and 2) that doing two things at once is better than just doing one. Worse, this ad literally puts words and flawed values into the mouths of children. Speed and multitasking are self-serving messages promoted by corporations; they are not words to live by.

I realize that the ad sponsors are just trying to sell smart phones, but they also reinforce misguided and dangerous cultural myths. Faster is better, I suppose, for a phone or an athlete. Some might recall another, wiser adage about speed: "Haste makes waste." Doing things quickly can mean doing them impulsively, shoddily, and without sufficient forethought. Examples of this kind of behavior abound in our culture where tactless, insensitive, and often counter-productive words or actions occur every day. This is especially true in politics, cyberspace, and all too often, in our daily encounters with people. It does not make us better people; it makes us free-floating egos and jerks—or worse, road ragers and murderers.

Wouldn't it be better instead to think before acting or speaking? How about doing things thoughtfully, deliberately, and well?

Is faster always better in nature? Consider birds. The House Sparrow is one of the most widespread, prolific bird species on earth. I have seen them in six different countries in two different hemispheres. Are they fast? No! Actually, they are among the slowest flying birds in the world. That's right; the House Sparrow can only fly 15-18 miles per hour, a speed that can be exceeded by human runners. In contrast, the Peregrine Falcon is the fastest bird in North America, capable of flying up to 175 miles per hour when stooping or descending upon its prey. Peregrines once were listed as Endangered Species in the U.S. and have since thankfully recovered to the point that they were removed from the Endangered Species list in 1999.

What about doing two or more things at once? Is this somehow better than doing one thing, as the ads suggest? Yes, if you want to be seen as a shallow, distracted individual—oblivious to the people and the environment around you. What happened to the belief that concentration, focus, and thoughtful consideration are desirable traits?

Most people are afraid to say the truth; that multitasking has been a dismal failure. As Susan Cain writes in her brilliant book, *Quiet: The Power of Introverts in a World That Can't Stop Talking,* "Another study, of 38,000 workers across different sectors, found that the simple act of being interrupted is one of the biggest barriers to productivity. Even multitasking, that prized feat of modern-day office workers, turns out to be a myth." It's true that we can do more than one thing at a time, but poorly. And while we are multitasking, we sometimes endanger others and ourselves, as when people text while driving.

Instead of blindly worshiping the false gods of speed and multitasking promoted by cell phone companies, let's be more thoughtful, deliberate, and focused. We will be more likely to survive and flourish this way. The quality of our lives and our relationships will improve too.

The Unfortunate Rake

Sadly, the yard and garden rake might be going the way of the broom and the push mower. What's wrong with the rake? Actually nothing; a lot is right with it. Rakes are great tools for a variety of yard work tasks, and as side benefits their rhythmic sound is gentle; they do not require fossil fuels or electricity; they do not emit air pollution other than a little dust; and we get exercise while using them. Studies and overwhelming visual evidence suggest that Americans need more, not less, exercise.

To counter the pro-rake crowd, of which I am one, I suppose pro-leaf blowers would say that rakes require too much effort and do not get as much done as quickly. Interestingly, I have noticed that yard services, using leaf blowers on yards comparable in size to mine with a similar amount of fallen leaves, run their blowers even longer than it takes me to rake our yard quite thoroughly.

But alas, it seems that most are going to the leaf blower. Progress in our culture often means burning fuels and running a motor. Anything to avoid running our human motor!

I heard Robert Pyle, renowned naturalist and author, refer to leaf blowers as "satanic devices." I agree. No thanks to leaf blowers, nearly every neighborhood in America, including ours, is dominated by their din, often for hours a day. Presumably leaf blowers perform a service by tidying up, removing leaves, and other yard debris. But actually, they often blow the debris somewhere else—into the street or into the yard of an adjacent business or neighbor. The two-stroke engine that powers many of them creates more pollution than many vehicles on the road today. The dust gets blown into the air, polluting our atmosphere. And the noise, the dreadful droning sound of leaf blowers, has made it thoroughly unpleasant to go outside. As if we needed yet another reason NOT to enjoy the outdoors! Leaf blowers cause more problems than they solve.

There is another factor at play, namely a sense of community. If you want to drive your neighbors away and prevent a conversation with them, turn on a leaf blower. If you would like to visit with them, use a hand rake. I have found that when I rake leaves in our yard, I often look up and engage neighbors or a random passer-by in conversation, which is nice. "The Unfortunate Rake" is an English folk song about a young soldier who faced a variety of maladies. Now things aren't looking so good for garden rakes. Here's hoping we keep our garden rakes, and enjoy the relative peace and quiet, fresh air, and exercise that accompany their use.

Creative Boredom

People who write often get asked: "Where do you get your ideas?" or "How do you overcome writer's cramp?" The answer to both is boredom. Boredom can be good. Yes, that's what I said. Sometimes when you do nothing, good ideas flow. This especially happens when you are outside walking, exercising (okay, that's not exactly doing nothing) and/or doing yoga (I know, you're not supposed to be thinking then).

Our culture fears boredom. We fight it vigorously by pumping in electronic entertainment, constant social engagement, keeping busy, shopping, or doing just about anything to protect ourselves from—well—ourselves and the sounds of silence. Try doing nothing. It has become a lost art.

I'm not suggesting that we drop out of society all of the time. I am suggesting that we drop out periodically, even regularly, for short periods of time. If we unplug, put down our iPhones, iPods, iPads, and laptops for a moment and look up, we just might encounter something special: nature, reflection, peace, and quite possibly, a creative thought!

Years ago, one of my daughters was given an assignment by her then fifth-grade teacher to sit outside quietly for one hour and write about her experience. "Impossible!" was her initial reaction to this assignment. But after she completed it, she ended up enjoying every minute of it.

It's good to embrace a little boredom now and then. And don't tell me you don't have time! Somehow people make time for TV shows, computer games, barhopping, Facebook, tweeting, texting, and all matter of things. People also say that they don't have time to read. Nonsense! I heard that Bill Clinton reads one hundred books a year. Are you busier than he is? I didn't think so. Make twenty minutes a week to be quiet, to be alone with your thoughts.

If you allow yourself to be quiet, to go outside, to get some exercise, to meditate, take yoga, or do some quiet, focused activity, you just might hear your inner voice. When you are relaxed and not multitasking or distracted by social posturing, then ideas can flow into your head. Often, that inner voice first raises worry thoughts, but once it gets past those, it comes through with good ideas. You cannot hear this voice most of the time, because it cannot penetrate the cultural din. First you have to turn off our noisy culture and all of its distractions. Once you do, boredom isn't so boring anymore, and you might have some creative ideas.

Natural Light Gathering

Greetings from the dark side of the planet. Here in the Northern Hemisphere, during the winter months, our sun is often a faint white glow, low on the horizon. It barely emits light, let alone heat. Come December 22, the Winter Solstice, the sun will be directly above the Tropic of Capricorn at 12 noon. This means the sun will be directly overhead at noon in places like Argentina, South Africa, and Australia. Meanwhile, here in the North Country, we will experience low angle lighting, dim at times, which, combined with clouds and storms, can make for gloomy conditions.

Do these gloomy conditions affect our moods? Absolutely. The appropriately named Seasonal Affective Disorder (SAD) results from low light conditions and is discussed at length by Dr. Norman Rosenthal in his book *Winter Blues*. My brother-in-law, Dr. Howard Cohen, briefly explained how SAD works: "Light comes into the eyes through the optic nerve, which tracks to the hypothalamus, which has much to do with emotions. The hypothalamus, located in our brain, connects the nervous system to the endocrine system via the pituitary gland. When there is not enough light, we become depressed, irritable, tired, and hungry." Sound familiar?

Those of us who live north of the Tropic of Cancer in places like the United States, Canada, Europe, the former Soviet Republic, and China are most susceptible to SAD. The farther north you live from the equator, the more likely you are to experience SAD. Light therapy is one of the key antidotes to SAD according to Dr. Rosenthal. Going outside into ambient light can make a big difference. Dr. Cohen, a psychiatrist, recommends this to his patients "all the time."

Looking at birds results in looking at the sky, which in turn, results in gathering light. But first you have to look up. You don't have to go anywhere special; your backyard or local park will do. If you have coastal areas, prairies, meadows, or wetlands nearby, so much the better. You will experience nature, gather light, and get exercise and fresh air—four uplifting sensations combined. My dermatologist reminds us, even in winter and especially at high elevations, to wear sunscreen and a hat.

Consider participating in an Audubon-sponsored Christmas Bird Count at this time of year. These one-day counts are offered in many countries in December and January. I lead one here in Seattle each year. They are a great way to meet people, learn about birds, see beautiful country, and gather light.

In the meantime, have a happy holiday season and a happy, light-infused hypothalamus!

Skies of November

"And the iron boats go as the mariners all know
with the gales of November remembered."
Gordon Lightfoot, The Wreck of the Edmund Fitzgerald.

Gloomy at times, frequently stormy, and tinged with magical light, the skies of November are breathtakingly beautiful. The play of low angle light against the backdrop of fast-moving storm clouds is absolutely entrancing. In this, the rainiest time of the year in Seattle, those who go outside, look up, or even peer skyward through a window are often rewarded. See one of the best free shows on earth.

Soul Refuges

Usually when we refer to refuges, we mean nature refuges. These are places rich in natural diversity, densely populated by birds and other forms of wildlife. They are often high in scenic value and provide a departure from our increasingly urban existence.

Refuges, however, are not just for bird and wildlife watchers, hunters, and fishermen. They are just as valuable for people who seek peace, beauty, contemplation, or a place to grieve.

Terry Tempest Williams in her perceptive novel *Refuge* wrote eloquently about the significance of nature refuges during a time of grieving. In her case, while her mother was struggling with cancer, she took periodic trips to the Great Salt Lake to regroup.

My wife went through this a few years ago with my then-ailing father-in-law. Her monthly visits were stressful, due to her efforts to balance financial, medical, legal, and organizational obligations with the quality time she needed to spend with her dad. Taking restorative walks at Dyke's Marsh along the

Potomac River helped her cope with this daunting situation.

At an event a decade ago, honoring my landscape architect/ park creator/conservationist great-grandfather, Jens Jensen, one speaker gave a powerful testimony to the value of parks as places to grieve. This high-level Chicago Parks Department official spoke passionately about the tragic loss of a family member and how he desperately needed a quiet, calming, and appropriate place to grieve. North Chicago's Humboldt Park, a Jens Jensen landscape, fulfilled this need.

All of us experience tragedies, letdowns, and eventually death. Where can we go to soothe our souls during these hard times? Natural areas—especially if we look up.

Look Up!

"Looking up from the flatlands, birds and clouds floating by … I'd say that heaven's a thousand feet high. It's my Home in the Sky, my home in the sky, hawk makes a circle through which swallows fly."
Greg Brown, "Home in the Sky"

Three days ago, I heard the familiar broken flute call of the Bald Eagle in my north Seattle backyard. I surveyed the tree tops to no avail, but then heard it again. This time I looked straight up and saw a Bald Eagle soaring, its wings flat and black against the blue sky. There was a lot of chattering for just one bird. Sure enough, soon I saw another, and another, until a total of five Bald Eagles were soaring over my house. A lot of people look down these days; at phones, iPads, and sometimes their feet. Perhaps they should receive a special Earth Day text message that encourages them to unplug and engage their senses instead. If they bothered to look up and listen they might notice something interesting—even inspiring.

Eagles are out in the spring, and so are Osprey, Turkey Vultures, a variety of hawks, and several species of swallows, along with many other bird species. Add to your daily enjoy-ment of life by checking out the sky. It's the greatest show above earth.

Chapter 3 - Restoring Landscapes

The Man Who Plants Native Trees and Plants

Jim Corson, trail steward extraordinaire
© Woody Wheeler

Fall graces Seattle's Burke-Gilman Trail with a canopy of yellow-green Bigleaf Maple leaves, some parachuting downward in lazy spirals. The smell of fresh, moist leaves is reminiscent of tea. Birds, including Bushtits, Chickadees, Kinglets and Juncos, forage through the trees and wild berry "crops." As I walk along, fifty or so people share this two-mile stretch with me during the hour I spend there. Several thousand people per day use this twelve-mile railroad right-of-way, one of Seattle's major bicycle/pedestrian corridors.

What is not immediately apparent is that the native vegetation along this stretch of trail is the result of a massive volunteer effort led by Jim Corson and the Friends of the Burke-Gilman Trail. His story is one of vision, hard work, and dedication, and demonstrates how one person can inspire others to make a difference.

Over the years, like many parks, this trail has also become a corridor for invasive plants such as English Ivy, Laurel, Himalayan Blackberry, Scot's Broom, and Holly. Left unattended, this area would eventually become a treeless landscape dominated by just a few species of invasive, non-native plants. The natural habitat and species diversity were already in serious decline until Jim Corson and Friends of the Burke-Gilman Trail got involved.

Friends of the Burke-Gilman formed in 2007 to restore native trees and plants, and to educate and involve the community in the stewardship of the Trail. Led by Jim, this group has transformed a two-mile segment of this urban bicycle and pedestrian trail corridor into a far more diverse natural landscape than it was when he started.

Jim, a retired clinical pharmacist from the University of Washington Medical Center, originally hails from Michigan. He became interested in restoration work when he saw a sign for a stewardship work party as he bicycled along the trail one day. He noticed the sign because he looked up from his bicycling. Jim volunteered and hasn't stopped since. Through Green Seattle Partnership Program, a public-private effort to re-establish and maintain healthy urban forests, Jim and his cadre of volunteers along with city crews have restored seven acres on a two-mile stretch of the Burke-Gilman Trail. Jim acknowledges the absolutely vital role that volunteers play in restoring the trail, "Without them, I'd still be working on the first mile."

Jim and the thousands of volunteers he has recruited over the years have planted more than five thousand trees, shrubs, and other native plants. He recruits volunteers from a wide variety of organizations including the University of Washington, the Girl Scouts, Seattle Public Schools, the EPA, Boeing, Microsoft, Starbucks, Amazon, and even the Tilted Thunder Roller Birds Team. He organizes about one hundred work parties per year; this from a man who is supposedly retired.

In addition to Jim and his crew's restoration efforts, there are educational activities, such as monthly bird walks to monitor the effects of restoration on bird species. These walks, which I lead, occur on the second Sunday morning of each month. Generally we see twenty to twenty-five species.

Landscape restoration, of the kind that Corson and his volunteers practice, is catching on. A number of other Washington State cities, including Everett, Kent, Kirkland, Tacoma, and Redmond have also started Green City partnership programs.

Doing so makes our cities more biologically diverse, beautiful, and ecologically stable. Interested? As Jim says "Along with enjoying the growth of a restored landscape, you wind up meeting really neat people, learning a lot, and leaving a little legacy." The last part is an understatement in his case!

Landscape Restoration Matters

When I worked at The Nature Conservancy in the 1990s, we were controlling invasive species and managing lands for their natural diversity. At the time, those of us engaged in this work felt lonely and overwhelmed by the scale of the problem. But a remarkable shift has happened since then, and it is being played out here in Seattle.

Landscape restoration has caught on in a big way—both locally and nationally. My daughter and I recently participated in several work parties along the Burke-Gilman Trail, where at least seven acres have been restored in the past five years. We pulled out blackberries, mulched the area with chips and cardboard, and later planted native trees and shrubs. It was satisfying work.

I see evidence of this kind of work all over town: from the Burke-Gilman Trail to Discovery, Lake People, Magnuson, Me-Kwa-Mooks, Ravenna, and Seward Parks. Madrona Woods, Jack Block Park, and Union Bay Natural Area are a few more places where people are actively restoring Seattle's natural diversity. It is not just happening here, restoration is occurring all over the world. I have witnessed it lately on former military bases, in county, state, provincial, and national parks, at airports, former landfills, and reclaimed hazardous waste sites, former industrial and agricultural areas. This trend is something to be proud of and to join in wherever possible.

As the late, great historian and author, Stephen Ambrose said, *"In the 19th Century we devoted our best minds to exploring nature. In the 20th Century we devoted ourselves to controlling and harnessing it. In the 21st Century the best minds are working on how to restore nature."* It all begins when you look up and notice the condition of the habitat. The next step is to do something about it. Participating in restoration is a tangible way to make the natural world more beautiful, resilient, and diverse.

A Circle of Life

A traffic circle transformed into a mini park
© Woody Wheeler

Our north Seattle neighborhood has the first and one of the largest traffic circles in the city. Over the years, it was taken over by invasive English Ivy and drug abusers who discarded their syringes and other drug paraphernalia in the thick ivy foliage.

Led by volunteers and backed by a Seattle Department of Neighborhoods grant, this traffic circle was transformed into a vital neighborhood green space. I became involved with this effort and was glad that I did. At a series of neighborhood work parties, volunteers pulled the ivy from the circle, then developed a planting plan that included a diverse array of native trees, shrubs, and wildflowers. They covered the circle with a thick layer of wood chip mulch to stabilize the site until the fall of 2010 planting season. At that time, a thousand native plants and four trees were planted by the thirty neighborhood volunteers who worked on the 5,500 square foot site. Since then, neighbors have watered, weeded, removed trash, and most importantly, enjoyed this vastly improved landscape.

Projects like this remind us that we can all positively impact the landscapes that surround us, and in so doing, improve the environment, our quality of life, and our relationships with neighbors.

Legalize Shrubs

Streetscape monoculture
© Woody Wheeler

Fully planted diverse streetscape
© Woody Wheeler

There is too much grass in the world—no, I'm not referring to the sometimes illegal kind, but rather the kind used for lawns, parks, golf courses, and many other landscapes. According to an article in *Conservation Weekly Dispatch*, "Residential lawns cover more of the United States than any other irrigated crop, and that includes the corn and soy that blanket the Midwest." What's wrong with this kind of grass? If you could ask Canada Geese, who are voracious grass eaters, nothing is wrong with it. But if you could ask salmon, plenty is wrong.

Grass is not inherently bad; it's the excessive use of fertilizers, chemicals, and water to create that golf-course look that creates problems. These run into our rivers, lakes, and oceans, causing water pollution. We can make our yards more diverse, more beautiful, and less toxic by landscaping them for wildlife habitat, food production, and natural diversity.

The median or planting strip—between the sidewalk and street—is a good place to start. As the pictures show, there is a marked contrast between a planted median strip and a plain grass lawn. One is inherently interesting and structurally diverse, and the other is a bleak monoculture.

While strolling down the sidewalk, you can eat apples from apple trees, watch birds, admire wildflowers, and enjoy fall colors from street trees—all from plantings in the median strip. One neighbor even has a bird bath hanging from his median strip tree. Another has a floral display worthy of a sidewalk wedding. There are many reasons to look up when walking by these rich and diverse median-strip landscapes.

Somewhere along the line, we learned as a society that grass was the norm for landscaping. Maybe it's time for a cultural shift to richer, more diverse, sustainable plantings. Check your local regulations before you start planting in your median strip.

Snagscaping

Wildlife tree occupied by Northern Flicker
© Christopher Moffett

Have a dead tree in your yard? Why not snagscape it into a wildlife tree?

Snags, or dead and dying trees, were formerly thought of as untidy and hazardous. But they have great ecological value and can be made safe. Russell Link, author of *Landscaping for Wildlife in the Pacific Northwest*, is decidedly pro-snagscaping: "Snags, along with other forms of rotting wood have tremendous value to wildlife: birds, flying squirrels, bats and other wildlife use snags for homes, nurseries, hunting territories and perching sites."

What is snagscaping anyway? Okay, I recognize it's not a well-known word. It means transforming a dead tree into a wildlife tree instead of removing it altogether. Here's how it works, courtesy once again of Russell Link: "By removing the top third of the tree along with about half of the remaining side branches, you will ensure that the tree begins the preferred inside-out decay process. You can also make the top look natural by creating a jagged top with a chain saw." Once the big limbs are removed, the hazard aspect is virtually gone, and then the snag becomes a home for woodpeckers and other cavity-nesting birds. Eventually it decomposes into the ground, enriching the soil.

Snagscaping is catching on. At Seattle's Magnuson Park, more than twenty "hazard" trees were salvaged from another city park, Seward Park, and inserted into the soil to become habitat snags as part of a major wetland restoration. The birds love them—especially raptors and woodpeckers. Seattle Audubon has an impressive wildlife snag in its original place right next to their office. We have one in our front yard. Many people stop, look up at it, and ask questions about it. At least two people have been inspired by it to create wildlife trees in their own yards. I have seen an ever-increasing number of other wildlife trees at city and state parks.

Small trees work for snagscaping too. As Link says,

"Red-breasted Nuthatches and Black-Capped Chickadees nest in snags as small as eight feet tall and eight inches in diameter."

Please DO try snagscaping at home, but hire professionals to do the pruning.

Tree Tolerance

Seattle is regarded as a progressive, tolerant city, but there is one type of resident that many Seattleites do not tolerate well: trees. Whenever a tree annoys someone for any reason, it seems that the tree comes down.

Despite its green reputation, Seattle is not faring so well with respect to trees. The average coverage for U.S. cities is 27 percent. However, according to a City Urban Forest Management Plan, in 2007 Seattle only had 18 percent coverage; down from 40 percent coverage in 1972. The plan calls for planting 600,000 trees by 2037 to restore Seattle's canopy to 30 percent. As of 2010, Portland, Oregon, had a 30 percent tree canopy in a city once nicknamed "Stumptown." Atlanta, Georgia, with 36 percent coverage was the top-ranked major U.S. city.

We need more not fewer trees. Trees provide beauty, habitat for birds and wildlife, shade, wind and erosion protection, clean air, and they mitigate climate change. According to a new report by the Green Cities Research Alliance, Seattle's trees "save the city about $23 million annually in carbon storage, pollution removal, and residential energy savings, and it would cost the city $4.9 billion to replace its trees."

Here are five reasons I've heard for felling trees, along with my comments. I hope you consider these as you make decisions on your property:

1. *"It's messy."* —Yes, all trees are messy to varying degrees. Curse the fact that we have to rake those gorgeous fall leaves; even though we need the exercise and fresh air, which trees help create!

2. *"It might fall on my house someday."* —This is often an exaggerated fear that an arborist can address. Determine the prevailing wind direction and assess the tree's health before opting to axe it. Instead of being destroyed, trees can be pruned or converted to wildlife habitat trees or snags to remove the hazard element while providing habitat values.

3. *"It's the wrong tree for this area."* —Translated, this usually means the owner intends to plant ornamental, "toy" trees, instead of our local native trees such as Douglas Fir, Western Red Cedar, and Western Hemlock. These native trees, when not too close to houses or utility lines, are actually the *right* trees for our area, specifically adapted to our soils and climate. As Seattle's reLeaf organization points out: "Large trees often become treasured neighborhood assets. Research has shown that they provide higher quality habitat for birds and other wildlife, and they have larger root systems to help stabilize hillsides and prevent erosion. Large trees do more to buffer weather conditions, providing shade on hot days to reduce the need for air conditioning, and blocking winter winds to help save on heating bills."

4. *"It blocks my view."* —Trees don't block views, they are views! Through trimming, you can retain or open up views beyond the trees. Views framed by trees are more beautiful than stark views with no vegetation in the foreground. Just ask nature photographers.

5. *"It blocks the sun."* —This could be a blessing in disguise. Shade keeps your house cool, which will become increasingly important as the climate continues to warm.

What happens when you clear-cut an entire neighborhood? This happened in the Ballard neighborhood of Seattle. Many of our early settlers liked their trees horizontal. Plus they made money that way and, as one of Seattle's flatter areas, Ballard was easy pickings for timber harvesting. Removing so many of Ballard's trees created a stark, barren urban landscape.

Since the 1990s there has been a vigorous effort to "Re-Tree Ballard." Trees are being restored, one household planting strip at a time. The city provides saplings to these residents at a substantially reduced rate. Hundreds of households have participated and many trees have been planted. Ballard has become a more desirable place.

If you don't have the opportunity to plant a tree in your yard, your local parks department, park foundation, or botanical garden might be able to help you. They often have tree donation programs that enable you to plant one in honor of a loved one. We planted trees in my mother's honor in Ravenna Park, Seattle, and the Chicago Botanic Garden through two of these programs.

Trees have been winning a few battles, but losing a war of attrition. All cities benefit when their trees and snags remain standing. Let's keep our trees vertical. They are invaluable not expendable natural assets. They give us many reasons to look up and enjoy the views, the colorful leaves and the birds and wildlife that they harbor.

Heavenly Landfill

Great Blue Heron at Montlake Fill, Seattle
© Woody Wheeler

Is it possible to enjoy good bird and wildlife-watching, great scenery, and even pleasant smells at a former city dump? The answer is an emphatic *yes*! Where? Union Bay Natural Area in Seattle *aka* Montlake Fill.

I was recently at the "Fill" on a glorious spring day. Mount Rainier loomed in the distance across Lake Washington. Tree Swallows darted into their nesting holes after their long journey from parts south. A Bald Eagle pair harassed the coots enroute to their massive nest. Virginia Rails *oinked* and *ka-dinked*, marsh wrens chattered noisily, and scores of Red-Slider Turtles basked on logs in the 60-degree weather. Black Cottonwood Trees perfumed the air with their intoxicating sweet aroma, one of the finest scents in nature.

This place was not always so nice. It was a city landfill until 1971 when it was capped and later became neglected, allowing a host of invasive plants to take over. Since the 1990s, the University of Washington and the Center for Urban Horticulture have used the site for restoration ecology. The results of their combined efforts are spectacular. Over two hundred species of birds now visit the "Fill" each year. It is rated one of the top birding destinations in Seattle, and was recently included on Audubon's new Puget Loop birding trail. In just a few hours on my last visit, I tallied forty species there. Native vegetation continues to be planted, while invasive species are removed by dedicated university students and volunteers. The habitat keeps improving.

The natural diversity there is very impressive for such an urban and previously compromised place. Located three miles from downtown Seattle, this seventy-four-acre refuge is just across the water from the University of Washington and its two sports stadiums. Sometimes, you hear the roar of the crowd and the marching bands playing at the Husky Football Stadium. If you look up, you might also see a Red-Tailed Hawk capturing a vole while that band is playing. I have.

This strange but wonderful refuge is a model for other similarly degraded sites. Most of our remaining landscapes are degraded to some extent. The fact that we can restore a literal dump into a natural area provides hope that we will transform other degraded landscapes.

Drum Solo Live at the Fill

Early spring light encourages birds to sing, and for some, to drum. On a recent spring day, Seattle's Union Bay Natural Area *aka* the Montlake "Fill" was alive with birds—my friend and I tallied forty-three species in two hours—including waterfowl, raptors, gulls, wrens, warblers, and sparrows, plus one plump beaver. Bird song filled the air. The aptly named Song Sparrow, as well as Bewick's Wren, Marsh Wren, and House Finch were among the most prominent singers.

For me, the highlight of the day occurred in the parking lot where a Northern Flicker perched atop a light fixture and proceeded to drum. By drumming, I mean it produced a series of short metallic drum rolls. As a former drummer, I found these amazing. It takes two hands, two sticks, and lots of practice for humans to perform smooth drum rolls. The Flicker did them with the equivalent of one hand and one stick (his bill). His rolls were smooth. Perhaps you've heard them on your stovepipe, roof vent, or chimney. Woodpeckers cannot sing, so they drum to attract mates and establish territory.

The next time you hear a woodpecker drum roll, try to appreciate it—which can be a bit difficult when it occurs at first light on your stovepipe. This is the song of wildlife in your neighborhood. It usually happens only during the spring time for a few months. After that, there should be no more drum solos until the next spring.

Urban Birding

Urban Bald Eagle
© Woody Wheeler

Would you attend an all-day birding trip on an industrial waterfront in a major city in the darkest, rainiest time of year? Would you even see any birds? On December 31, 2011, five intrepid birders joined me for this very trip. It was Seattle Audubon's Annual Christmas Bird Count. The origins of these counts date back to the late 1800s when people in the U.S. took part in an annual tradition called the "Christmas Side Hunt." This was a competition to shoot the most birds possible in a day. The side that had the biggest pile of dead birds at the end of the day won.

In 1900, ornithologist and early Audubon Society office Frank Chapman proposed an alternative tradition: The Christmas Bird Count. It has since become the longest-running citizen science survey of birds in the world. Currently, tens of thousands of volunteers participate in this count in more than 2,300 count circle areas. In these counts, each team counts the total number of species as well as the number of individuals of each species. The 2013 Seattle Audubon Christmas Count for example tallied 123 species and 48,000 individual birds. Our count circle encompassed a two-mile stretch of Seattle's heavily-developed Shilshole Bay, from Golden Gardens Park to the Ballard Locks and Fisherman's Wharf. We tallied 67 species of birds, 18 California Sea Lions, and one River Otter. Among our less common findings were: Orange-Crowned and Townsend's Warbler; Thayer's and Herring Gull; Common Murre, Harlequin Duck, and a Pacific Loon.

In fairness, there were extenuating circumstances that led to this relatively high species count. First, I was accompanied by five competent birders, two of them armed with spotting scopes. Secondly, since this was the Christmas Bird Count, we worked hard to count every species and bird. Third, we had incredibly good weather for this time of year: clear, calm, dry, sunny, and nearly 50 degrees—atypical for Seattle in December.

Another factor was at play too: habitat. Although most of our route consisted of marinas, shipyards, restaurants, railroads, and condos, we spotted the majority of the birds and wildlife at Golden Gardens Park. This park features native vegetation and two shallow ponds bordered by riparian vegetation that are packed with wintering waterfowl, especially Mallards, American Wigeons, Buffleheads, and Northern Shovelers. The upper portion of the park is a wooded hillside with tall evergreens and snags that provide habitat for Bald Eagles, other raptors, and woodpeckers.

As I've noticed before on Christmas counts in Seattle, Tacoma, Walla Walla, Marysville, and other urban locations, habitat is absolutely the key to bird abundance and diversity. Parkland and green space areas with high bird activity contrast sharply with less-vegetated neighborhoods nearby that might host only a handful of species, such as American Crows, House Sparrows, House Finches, and European Starlings.

Fortunately, many cities have been improving their urban landscapes of late to make them greener and more diverse. Seattle is among them, with its Green Seattle Partnership program, and numerous other public and private restoration efforts. Since most of us live in cities, green spaces are absolutely vital. They literally help us breathe more easily by providing oxygen, and, as many studies have shown, they relieve stress. They also provide homes for birds and wildlife, which in turn enrich our lives.

Chapter 4 - Conserving Our Best Assets

Shopping by Bike

Many car trips in the United States are less than one mile, a readily bikeable or walkable distance. Yet, some of us drive our ton or heavier vehicles and burn fossil fuels just to travel those few blocks. There are better ways to go. Cities like Seattle are starting to promote non-car alternatives.

I hate shopping, but biking makes it not only tolerable but fun. You get exercise, and you experience the simple pleasure of cruising around in the open air, including up and down hills. When you look up, you see all kinds of people; you experience the wind, the weather, the birds and wildlife, the changes in seasons, the interesting yards, landscapes, buildings, and other surroundings in your neighborhood. At the end of the trip, you feel good, as opposed to drained or lethargic from that same car trip.

Mike Royko, the late great Chicago columnist, used to lampoon a mythical lazy American prototype he called "Rollin' Wheels." Rollin' never went anywhere "without steel belted radials underneath him." It's time to substitute two bicycle tires or our own two feet for the steel-belted radials. If you insist upon having big wheels beneath you, take public transit. The planet and your health stand to benefit.

Tri-Errand-Athlon

In this competition-obsessed country, there are winners and losers, but mostly losers. Trophies, championships, and accolades go to the relative few. Oddly, our athletic events seem divorced from our daily lives. Aside from those who commute to work by bicycle, on foot, or via transit, we don't seem to integrate exercise well into our daily routines. Here is an "event" that anyone in reasonable health can enjoy. Each time you participate in it, both you and the Earth win. This is how it works: the next time you need to run errands within two miles of your home, do them on foot or by bicycle instead of by car. If you run three errands, you just completed a Tri-errand-athlon.

I can already hear the litany of excuses:

- I'm too old for this (I'm 62).
- Our weather is often bad (ours is usually bad).
- We have hills (so do we, big time, courtesy of the glaciers).
- I've got bad knees (I could enter a bad-knee competition—I have had three surgeries!)
- I don't have time (it can be just as fast to walk or bike when you factor in traffic and parking).
- The businesses where I run errands are too far away (okay, this is valid, but only if you are talking about them being MILES distant).

Excuses aside, here's how it works. Several days ago, I got on my bike, rode one mile on a cloudy, drizzly 40-degree day. My first errand was to drop off our tax return with an accountant. Then I rode to the drug store and bought a few items to stow in my bike panniers—storage bags attached to my bike. The third errand was to the grocery store where I bought quite a few items, which, combined with the other stuff I'd bought, added up to forty pounds total. The items included a gallon of milk, a dozen eggs, a bag of apples, a bunch of bananas, two containers of berries, and two loaves of bread. They all fit in my two bike panniers and one small backpack, and they all made it home intact. This was my athletic "feat" of the day—a successful Tri-errand-athlon completed in one hour's time. And I ride slowly.

I challenge you to complete a tri-errand-athlon of your own. You can easily surpass my accomplishments of three stops, forty pounds of goods, and two miles completed in one hour. Regardless of whether or not you top my marks, you win every time you get on a bike or walk instead of getting in a car. Why? You get exercise, and when you look up, you experience the great outdoors. You also save on money and gas, and you have fun. Good luck on your Tri-errand-athlon! I'm off on another one right now.

Small is Still Beautiful

In 1973, British economist E.F. Schumacher wrote the book *Small is Beautiful.* It challenged the myth that bigger is better and Schumacher was an early adopter of the sustainability movement. Now, almost a half-century later, we still talk sustainability but struggle with implementation. Until recently, we have been backsliding in the United States.

Our houses are bigger—the average American home in 2009 had 2,065 square feet, up from about 1,400 square feet in 1970, according to the National Association of Home Builders.

Our cars are bigger—"Vehicles Keep Inching Up and Putting on Pounds"—*USA Today,* 2007. Why are we inexorably drawn to super sizes? What does seeking "bigger is better" do for us? Not much.

We consume more energy and spew excess air pollution to power our big cars and homes.

We fight wars to maintain the fossil fuel supply.

We postpone serious efforts to develop renewable energy and conservation measures.

Can we do better? Yes, when we collectively want to or have to. In recent years, a down economy and the price of gasoline finally, resulted in car manufacturers building and marketing more fuel-efficient cars. For the first time in decades, good gas mileage has become an important factor in a car-buying decision. Companies like Ford and GM boast about their fleet of cars that get thirty MPG or better.

In 2011, *Bloomberg Business* and *Financial News* reported:

> "The (Chevy) Cruze was the best-selling U.S. compact
> in July at 24,648 cars. GM has found the sweet spot in
> the market, pricing the Cruze at as little as $16,525,
> between the Corolla and the Prius, and delivering
> mileage of 30 mpg or more. GM produces the Cruze at
> its Lordstown, Ohio, plant, which employs 4,150 hourly
> workers and 350 salaried employees, according to the
> company's website. GM added 1,200 jobs to the factory
> last year for a third shift."

Fuel efficiency + increased car sales + new jobs = a promising formula that other U.S. and foreign car manufactures can replicate. Small can indeed be beautiful.

Missed "InVestas" Opportunities

Wind power is finally gaining traction in the United States. We recently passed Germany to become the nation producing the most wind power. Up to 20 percent of our nation's electricity could be generated by wind power by 2030.

While this is encouraging news, we in the United States were late to the table, and missed business opportunities because of it. Powerful oil and gas lobbyists and conservative politicians retarded our nation's investment in conservation and alternative energy at an opportune time. Ronald Reagan dismantled the Solar Energy Research Institute in 1980, which had been started by his predecessor, Jimmy Carter. President Carter unsuccessfully tried to sound the alarm for an energy crisis in the late 1970s and the need to move toward conservation, efficiency, and renewable energy sources. We did not listen.

Meanwhile, Danish wind-turbine manufacturer Vestas and the country of Denmark took action. The *Times* Science article

"How Denmark Sees the World in 2012" stated that "Denmark is a world leader in wind energy, and produces more than 10 percent of its power from turbines. That's meant cleaner air and greener jobs. The homegrown wind company Vestas is a world leader earning $8 billion a year, an impressive figure in a country that has barely half the population of Hong Kong." Even *Fox News* acknowledged in a 2006 story that "Denmark Points Way in Alternative Energy.... America has been outclassed, and by an unlikely competitor. In the realm of alternative energy, there is an inconspicuous European nation that could stand to teach the U.S. a few lessons—Denmark."

According to the Vestas website: "In the 1970s during the second oil crisis, Denmark's Vestas Company began to examine the potential of the wind turbine as an alternative source of clean energy. Vestas began producing wind turbines in 1979" (vestas.com).

Due to our nation's slow response to the energy crises, we missed business, environmental, and energy conservation opportunities. In 2014, Vestas' wind turbines yielded 19 percent of the global installed base of wind-energy output. Here in the state of Washington, at least two hundred Vestas turbines are in operation at wind farms. The installed price of each commercial wind turbine is approximately $3.5 million. Granted, Vestas has U.S. assembly plants, including facilities in Oregon and Colorado, and buys U.S. made materials for its turbines, but the point is a Danish company capitalized on this worldwide market because the U.S. had its head, metaphorically, in the oil sands.

As for the U.S., we are finally getting on track more than thirty years after Carter's Energy Crisis speech. According to the American Wind Energy Association, "Growth of wind power was helped by a federal stimulus package that extended a tax credit and provided other investment incentives for the industry." This is the kind of government leadership we need:

one that bolsters energy security, conservation of natural resources, and reduces the chance that we will get drawn into oil
wars.

Wind energy does have environmental impacts. As a bird
guy, you might wonder why I support it. The biggest bird kill-
ers, however, are house cats, who kill 2.4 billion birds a year,
and building windows, with a toll of up to 970 million birds
per year. Wind turbines kill 150,000-200,000 birds per year. At
the wind farm that we visited, one to two birds per turbine are
killed each year. While these bird fatalities are not good, they
are a reasonable trade-off given the environmental and political
consequences of other forms of energy production. The perfect
is the enemy of the good.

Audubon "strongly supports properly sited wind power as a
clean alternative energy source that reduces the threat of global
warming. Wind power facilities should be planned, sited, and
operated to minimize negative impacts on bird and wildlife
populations." I concur.

Rock Rabbits on the Run

Pika
© John Carlson

Heard any Pikas lately in the mountains? Seen any? The next time you are in the high country, look up and listen carefully. This adorable alpine mammal, which resembles and in fact is a miniature rabbit, inhabits western U.S. and Canadian mountain talus slopes. It announces its presence with a loud nasal "beep" or "eenk" and is heard more often than seen.

As the global atmosphere warms, the American Pika *aka* Rock Rabbit or Coney is becoming imperiled. Pikas are heat intolerant. According to a recent *Scientific American* article, it only takes six hours of 77-degree-plus weather to kill them. To cope with increasing heat, Pikas may be forced to higher and higher elevations, possibly leading to their extinction.

Pikas need to be outdoors in the summer "haying." They gather stockpiles of vegetative matter to feed on during the long months of the year spent underground. By mixing in a few toxic, rot-resistant plants, Pikas help preserve their hay piles during the long winter. In addition to the heat, Pikas need to fear a host of predators, including eagles, hawks, coyotes, bobcats, foxes, weasels, and dogs.

Four years ago, there was a failed attempt to have Pikas added to the Endangered Species List. Let's not allow these charming, niche-specific critters to literally fall through the cracks. Losing them would make the mountains a lonelier, less diverse, and less ecologically stable place.

Grizzly Nutcracker Tree

What dietary preference do Grizzly Bears and Clark's Nutcrackers share? Both consume large quantities of Whitebark Pine seeds. Clark's Nutcrackers rely heavily upon them, while grizzlies seek them as one of their most important fall foods, high in protein and fat. Red Squirrels and Black Bears also feed on these seeds.

Grizzlies feed on Whitebark Pine seeds from mid-August to late fall. Sometimes they dig up Red Squirrel caches of cones to obtain a larger supply—even when there is up to six feet of snow. Female grizzlies especially rely upon the high-energy seeds of the Whitebark Pine to build up their fat reserves prior to hibernation.

Unfortunately, these high-energy nuts are in decline, along with the tree that produces them. The ramifications of this tree's decline are far reaching, including changes in snowmelt volume, changes in alpine plant and animal diversity in alpine areas, and more grizzly/human encounters as Grizzlies forage in human space for food. Whitebark Pines grow on windy ridges in mountainous areas. If you look up while hiking on alpine ridges, you will see their bonsai-like wind-sculpted forms. True to their name they have whitish bark along with needles in bundles of five. They are beautiful trees found in beautiful environments.

The ecological values of Whitebark Pines are many. They act as snow fences, causing large accumulations of snow, which later result in delayed snow melt, which leads to longer periods of ephemeral stream flows. They provide vegetative cover where otherwise there is little to none, and they provide nutritious seeds to feed birds and mammals.

Whitebark Pines are declining rapidly in the northern Rockies. The hardest hit areas are near Yellowstone and Glacier National Parks. Their decline is primarily due to warming temperatures that enable the Mountain Pine Beetle to survive through the winter and to exist at higher elevations. This spells disaster for the Whitebark Pines. By 2009, 90 percent of these alpine trees in the Greater Yellowstone Ecosystem showed significant beetle activity. Grizzly expert and advocate Doug Peacock said in an interview by *Yale Environment 360* that "82-83% of the Whitebark Pines in the Greater Yellowstone Ecosystem are either dead or dying."

What can be done about this? Biologists are attaching packets of Verbenone (a synthetic pheromone that deters beetles) to Whitebark trees that demonstrate high cone production and resistance to disease. Seeds are also being collected from disease-free trees to test them for genetic resistance. A recent attempt to place the Whitebark Pine under protection under the *Endangered Species Act* failed. The U.S. Fish and Wildlife Service said that it will not immediately list the tree, due to higher priorities and a lack of funding. It may or may not revisit this decision.

In the meantime, along with the tree's demise, we will likely witness a decrease in the Clark's Nutcracker population and an increase in human/grizzly encounters. When Doug Peacock was asked if the loss of pine nuts was going to result in more contacts between bears and humans, he replied, "Absolutely, absolutely."

On one of my recent tours that passed through Cooke City, Montana on the northeast border of Yellowstone Park, I encountered evidence that this is already occurring. The town bakery we visited had had a grizzly at its doorstep earlier the same morning. According to the store proprietor, another grizzly had taken several steps into the bakery on a previous visit before retreating. Ironically, this bakery sold "Bear Claws." Be prepared to meet more of your grizzly neighbors if you live in the Greater Yellowstone Ecosystem.

Tanager Tree

Western Tanager
© Jeff Larsen

The month of May is a great time of year to observe birds and bird migration in North America. Look up at the tree tops, watch for movement, and listen for bird songs—particularly the "chid-up" call of tanagers. Watch for a flash of bright color.

The charismatic and colorful Western Tanager is a late spring arrival to the Western U.S. and Canada. For those of you who live in eastern North America, you might see the brilliant Scarlet Tanagers or, in the Midwest, southern and southeastern U.S., the Summer Tanagers. Those of you in the southwest can watch for Hepatic Tanagers and Summer Tanagers migrating north. All of these tanagers are all absolutely stunning with striking, colorful plumage.

I call one large Douglas Fir tree visible from my backyard the "Tanager Tree." That is because six Tanagers were in the top of it as I wrote this essay. This was not a one-time occurrence; it's a popular stopping place every year during their spring and fall migrations.

According to backyard lists I have kept since 1993, Tanagers arrive in my yard between May 1 and 18. This year the date was May 7. They are remarkably consistent in the timing of their journey from Mexico. Even more remarkable is the sight of them in the top of the exact same Douglas Fir tree each year.

This type of behavior is called *philopatry*, a term for site fidelity. Many birds return annually to specific stopping points like these during their migratory journeys. A Harlan's Hawk that winters in Washington's Skagit Valley perches on the very same pole there each year.

Western Tanagers breed in the coniferous forests of the Cascade foothills, but a few of them stop and perch in the same north Seattle Douglas Fir on the way there and on their way back to Mexico. I am always grateful to hear the harsh "chid-up" call, and to see their bright yellow and red forms, like Christmas tree ornaments. Keep an eye and an ear out; they could be passing through the tops of your neighborhood trees.

Working the Sap Lines

Red-breasted Sapsuckers at nest hole
© Gregg Thompson

Hardly anyone notices it, yet the Red-Breasted Sapsucker is often right there next to a moderately busy sidewalk, perhaps twelve feet up a Sweet Gum tree. You can see its handiwork even when it is not around: parallel rows of sap lines or wells. I refer to "it" because distinguishing gender in this species is very difficult. The Sapsucker goes about its business, seemingly oblivious to passers-by, traffic, construction crews across the street, or people like me taking pictures of it.

Fortunately, a Red-Breasted Sapsucker chose to harvest a Sweet Gum tree located in our front yard. It drills and feeds there for hours at a time, mostly silently, occasionally making a soft tapping sound.

Red-Breasted Sapsuckers, like their cousins, the Red-Naped, Williamson's and Yellow-Bellied Sapsuckers belong to the woodpecker family. The range of Red-Breasted Sapsuckers follows the west coast of North America from Baja California, Mexico to southeast Alaska. They drill sap holes or wells, drink the sap, and eat the tree's inner bark and the insects that become trapped in the sap that flows from their wells. Other birds benefit from their work, too, especially hummingbirds, which also eat the sap and trapped insects.

The colorful Red-Breasted Sapsucker goes about its business each day, bringing joy to those who notice it at work, and food to other species of birds. Last winter, its tree was damaged by a windstorm. Afterward, some considered it dead and unsightly. We had it trimmed so that it resembles a wildlife tree or snag, only it still lives. Like the other wildlife tree in our yard, it provides valuable food and habitat for birds. Now that it remains standing, it is a feeding place for the Red-Breasted Sapsucker. What an amazing yet brilliant ecological niche this species occupies! You notice things like this when you look up and listen.

Hermit Revival

Sometimes wildlife adventures happen close to home. One day several years ago, a Hermit Thrush crashed into my neighbor's window.

I found the thrush sprawled out on the ground, conscious but barely moving. Gently, I picked up the small, nearly weightless bird and cradled it between my hands to warm it and help alleviate the shock. I intended to place it in a small box and leave it in a quiet place, away from pets and predators. This is the recommended treatment for window-stunned birds. But before I could transfer it to the box, the thrush stood up on my hand. It perched briefly before fluttering to the ground beneath a nearby shrub. There it stood motionless. My neighbor and I watched the bird closely, ready to fend off any prowling cats.

An hour later, the thrush flew up to the fence, then across my yard to my Evergreen Huckleberry bush, where it eagerly ate the berries. It had recovered!

Hermit Thrushes breed in the coniferous forests of the Cascade and Rocky Mountains and all across Canada, clear up into Alaska. They winter in the Puget Sound lowlands in areas with berries and dense brush, like our native-plant landscaped backyard. Their name derives from their reclusive lifestyle of foraging for insects and berries on the forest floor. The song of the Hermit Thrush is so hauntingly beautiful that David Sibley, author of *The Sibley Guide to Birds*, once said at a local book reading event that he regarded it as his favorite.

Watch for their rusty-red rump and heavily-spotted chest. They stand proudly upright with their head held high. This thrush definitely looks up! Our revived thrush will hopefully be singing its resonant flute-like song in the Cascade Mountains next summer.

Saving Sacred Lands

More than four million people visit Yellowstone and Grand Teton National Parks annually. Drawn by amazing scenery, wildlife, and geysers, tourists from all around the world flock to these incredible parks. Just stand around Old Faithful Geyser and listen to the chorus of foreign languages as people watch its regular eruptions. What millions of tourists from the U.S. and many other countries realize is that these are sacred lands in a world where nature has not only been tamed, but often destroyed.

Last summer, I was fortunate to be a guide for Heatherlea Expeditions from Scotland in partnership with U.S-based Naturalist Journeys to tour these two parks and their adjacent National Forests and Refuges. On our tour, because we looked up often, we saw more than 140 species of birds and at least a dozen species of mammals, including bison, Black and Grizzly Bears, Northern Gray Wolf, coyote, Mule Deer, Pronghorn Antelope, mountain goats, Pika, and River Otter. We not only saw these birds and animals; we saw them at close range interacting with one another. The species abundance and diversity in this area is not coincidental. It is due to the enormous area and the quality of the natural habitat set aside by visionary politicians (not always an oxymoron) from years past.

Together, Yellowstone and Grand Teton Parks comprise 2.5 million acres. What makes these parks even better as wildlife and ecological reserves is that they are contiguous to seven National Forests and three National Wildlife Refuges. The sum total of all these areas is over twenty million acres of connected natural landscapes, also known as the Greater Yellowstone Ecosystem.

Three Rs were key to preserving these sacred lands: Teddy Roosevelt, Franklin Delano Roosevelt, and John Rockefeller. Teddy Roosevelt, with the capable assistance of Gifford Pinchot, established National Forests and National Wildlife Refuges. John Rockefeller purchased 35,000 acres of land between the two parks and held it for fifteen years until Grand Teton Park was finally approved. FDR's pocket veto of a bill opposing "Jackson Hole National Park" allowed this to happen. Finally in 1950, Harry Truman signed the bill merging Rockefeller's 35,000 acres with the rest of the park.

Filmmaker Ken Burns referred to National Parks as "America's best idea." Public lands such as National Forests, National Monuments, and Wildlife Refuges were great ideas too. We all know what would have happened to these lands without these designations. They would be privatized, developed, and cleared of most wildlife, as the lands surrounding them have been cleared. It is worth noting that the three Rs included a Republican, a businessman, and a Democrat. Are there leaders today with the backbone, vision, and collaborative spirit to protect sacred lands for future generations? As Teddy Roosevelt, the best-ever conservation president in the U.S. said, "The nation behaves well if it treats the natural resources as assets which it must turn over to the next generation increased, and not impaired, in value." (Theodore Roosevelt, 1910)

Roosevelts Won Olympics

Several years ago, my family and I hiked the spectacular Ozette Triangle in Olympic National Park. We were awed by its beauty and the abundance and diversity of its wildlife. At Sand Point alone, by looking up we spotted multiple Bald Eagles, Great Blue Herons, Black Oystercatchers, Harlequin Ducks, shorebirds, gulls, sea otters, seals, sea lions, deer, and raccoons; not to mention the uncountable number of tide pool dwellers.

Our hike included three of the seventy-three miles that you can walk along pristine Pacific coastline. We were grateful for this experience, and sang the praises of those who made it possible—most notably, the Roosevelts.

Theodore Roosevelt (TR) established Mount Olympus National Monument in 1909, primarily to protect elk habitat. His fifth cousin, Franklin Delano Roosevelt (FDR), elevated the area to National Park status in 1938. The U.S. Congress finished the job by adding the coastal strip of Olympic National Park to the national system of Wilderness areas in 1988.

The vision and leadership of the Roosevelts has left us an incredible legacy of unspoiled temperate rainforests, beaches, sea stacks, tide pools, and wildlife. Many thanks TR and FDR!

A Tale of Two Middle Forks

Flash back to fifteen years ago. Two families, including ours, went on a Fourth of July hike on a beautiful summer day to the Middle fork of the Snoqualmie River, a semi-wild area, thirty-five miles east of Seattle. Five young kids were involved in this hike. By the end of it, we were worried about their safety and all of our lives.

We parked at the Middle Fork Trailhead, hiked into the old-growth woods along the river for a few miles, and that's when the shooting began. It was not just an idle gunshot, nor was it Fourth of July fireworks. Multiple rounds of gunshots fired close by seemed more like a battle than target shooting. We gathered our families, keeping low to the ground, and hustled out, half-expecting bullets to come whistling through the vegetation. It was like being in a war zone.

That was the Middle Fork of old, a place of neglect, abuse, shooting galleries, meth labs, garbage, cars in the river, and worse. It was a family-hostile place and an insult to the quality of nature that exists there. All of this was located between the Alpine Lakes Wilderness Area and the rapidly developing suburban city of North Bend, Washington, just forty-five minutes from Seattle.

Now flash forward to yesterday. It was another beautiful summer day, but this time, our hiking experience was much different. We went again as a family with our now college-aged daughter. We saw many other families there, including parents with toddlers. We heard the rushing sound of the Middle Fork of the Snoqualmie River, along with the calls and songs of twenty-plus bird species. We looked up and saw a spectacular setting of temperate old-growth forest with stunning views of Mount Garfield and the central Cascade Mountains behind. No gunshots were fired this time and no conspicuous garbage or neglect marred the views. Instead, attractive, informative interpretive signs welcomed hikers and bikers to the trail head, and many people hiked, picnicked, fished, and enjoyed the beautiful area. Washington Trails Association volunteers improved the already well-maintained trails.

One would never know what this area had been like before. Thank goodness! This has been nothing short of a transformation—a public lands triumph brought about by a major state designation of a new conservation area four years ago. The culture of land use has changed for the better.

In 2009, Washington State Land Commissioner, Peter Goldmark, announced a new 10,720-acre Natural Resources Conservation Area (NRCA) in the Middle Fork Valley. "I have designated this new Middle Fork Natural Resources Conservation Area which has higher elevation old forests and connects valuable wildlife corridors across a broad landscape. In addition, the new NRCA will offer scenic views and low impact public use."

This type of conservation vision and leadership can and should be replicated on the national and international stages.

Happy 150th Jens Jensen

Mahoney Park sign
© Woody Wheeler

Jens Jensen Council Ring in Mahoney Park
© Woody Wheeler

September 13, 2010 was Jens Jensen's 150th birthday. No, this renowned landscape architect, maker of parks, conservationist, and great-grandfather of mine was not still alive then, but at least three celebrations were held that year in his honor: one was in Ellison Bay, Wisconsin at The Clearing; a second was in Chicago, Illinois; and a third took place at his birthplace in Dybbol, Denmark. I attended the Ellison Bay 150th birthday and 75th anniversary of the Clearing—a wonderful event that drew two hundred or more people—at the school that he established. Here is a piece that I read at the event:

A tribute to my Great Grandfather, Jens Jensen
By Woody Wheeler, May 2009

Sometimes I wish I had been born five years earlier. Then I could have walked with my great-grandfather, Jens Jensen. Dad wrote about such walks, "As a boy he was fun to be with. On walks through the woods he would point out Lady Slippers, Indian Pipes, and other plants that I would never have noticed. He said that Kinnikinnick, a ground cover, was used by the Indians for tobacco. It was fascinating to go with him."

Jens Jensen was at least sixty years ahead of his time. He was totally "green" long before the current meaning of this word had even been conceived.

He was green at a time when the fashionable way of thinking was gray, as in pavement, as in industry, as in rapid progress and development. Nature was to be conquered and dominated, not cherished. As John Graf said in his book *Images of Chicago's Parks*, "His (Jens Jensen's) belief that the city and park designs be harmonious with nature became a major theme in American landscape design long before environmental activists spoke out."

During these times, Jens Jensen designed landscapes with native plants. Many of his clients resisted; they wanted exotic plants. Native plants were considered pedestrian and unremarkable. Jensen persisted, and showed through his parks, estates, rock walls, waterfalls, and other landscapes, just how gorgeous a native prairie could be. He convinced people that prairies were worthy of preservation. This was far from conventional wisdom in his time and required great force of character, which, based on all accounts, Jens Jensen had in abundance.

You get a taste of Jens Jensen's determination and persuasive powers in his book *Siftings*, where he wrote, "It is often remarked native plants are coarse. How humiliating to hear an American speak so of plants with which the Great Master has decorated his land!"

Finally, more than sixty years later, his ideas have gained traction. His unconventional wisdom has become conventional. His ideas are now taught in college landscape architecture classes, they are practiced by conservation organizations, by state and federal agencies; they are featured in museum exhibits, at interpretive displays and chronicled in books. They are applied to the stewardship of parks and natural areas, including at some he helped establish such as Indiana Dunes State Park and the Chicago Forest Preserve system, now called the Chicago Wilderness.

Thanks in part to Jens Jensen's leadership there are now native plant societies and nurseries; people are planting native plants in yards, parks, state and national parks—and attempting to control exotic, invasive plants. As a society, we are finally beginning to grasp the importance of native plants to our ecology. In today's lexicon, native plants are considered to be sustainable components of our natural heritage and its biological diversity.

Although Jens Jensen was well known for his city park projects and privately landscaped estates, he also helped preserve an extensive network of native prairie, wetland, and forest lands: the Forest Preserve system in Cook County, Illinois. This interconnected landscape, now referred to as the Chicago Wilderness, extends for more than fifty miles along Chicago's western fringe. It has become a national model for preserve design and is one of Illinois' largest natural areas.

In addition to the Chicago Wilderness, Jens Jensen, the Prairie Club, and Friends of Our Native Landscape saved other native landscape gems such as the Indiana Dunes, now an Indiana State Park; and White Pines, and Starved Rock, now both Illinois State Parks. At the behest of Jensen, a moving outdoor masque entitled "Beauty in the Wild" was written by Kenneth Sawyer Goodman and performed at proposed nature reserves in the Midwest in the early 1900s. This helped inspire people to protect these and other places that are now state parks. My sister, Jensen Wheeler, directed the revival performances of "Beauty in the Wild" in Chicago's Columbus Park and at the Clearing in Ellison Bay, Wisconsin, in 1992. I had the distinct pleasure of seeing the Clearing masque.

Jens Jensen believed that people need to tend gardens, to get in touch with the soil, and to be taught to respect and admire the natural world. That is why he founded the Clearing in 1935, a school in Ellison Bay, Wisconsin dedicated to the environment, humanities, and the arts; it still operates today.

I never met Great-Grandfather Jensen—he died one month before I was born—but he has profoundly influenced my life. My work for the past thirty years for the Nature Conservancy, Audubon, Seattle Parks Foundation, and now as a nature tour guide, was inspired by him.

Last year, my wife and I replaced the grass in our backyard with more than a hundred native plants. Maybe Jens Jensen made us do this. If so, we are glad that we did; so are the neighbors and birds.

I wish that I had met him and I'm sure that many others feel this way too. In the meantime, we can all do things to make him proud. As Robert Grese said in his wonderful book: *Jens Jensen, Maker of Natural Parks and Gardens*, "Today the potential exists to carry Jensen's vision much further." In Jens Jensen's own words, "Everyone is entitled to a home where the sun, the stars, open fields, giant trees, and smiling flowers are free to teach an undisturbed lesson of life. Herein lies my task." Let us all commit to carrying on this noble task in his honor.

Note: For those interested in learning more about Jens Jensen, a documentary film about him was released in 2013 entitled: *Jens Jensen, The Living Green* by Carey Lundin, Viva Lundin Productions.

A Forest Grows in Bothell

Forest Friends—Carolyn Freese and Jeanie Robinson
© Woody Wheeler

*"Prize the natural spaces and shorelines most of all, because
once they're gone, with rare exceptions
they're gone forever."*
Richard Louv, *Last Child in the Woods*

Imagine a large forested wetland with mature native trees, abundant flora and fauna in the middle of a fast-growing suburban city near Seattle. This green space connects to a creek, then a river that flows into Lake Washington and, via a ship canal, to Puget Sound, providing a functioning salmon stream. Are we dreaming here? No. Remarkably, such a place still exists: The North Creek Forest in Bothell, Washington, a city of thirty-thousand-plus people.

Located just a mile from City Hall in northeastern Bothell, North Creek Forest encompasses 63.8 acres of undeveloped mature coniferous forest with nine distinct wetlands. It forms a one-mile long and one-third-mile-wide corridor extending from Canyon Park Junior High in the north to the North Creek wetlands by the University of Washington Bothell Campus, and eventually to the Sammamish River. This green belt directly benefits fish, wildlife, birds, and the people who frequent the area. In addition, it provides less obvious but substantial "free public services" such as clean air, carbon dioxide absorption, fresh water, flood control, and soil stabilization.

Since 2000, The Friends of North Creek Forest have worked tirelessly to protect this land. Toward this end of last year, they obtained a Conservation Futures grant from King County. Two individual friends of the forest have since purchased six acres in the central portion of the forest to save it from development. The long-term goal is to safeguard the entire 63.8-acre natural area so that it remains a major green space for the benefit of Bothell's citizens and others in the region.

Bothell's slogan is *"Bothell, a great place to live."* Bothell is currently undergoing a downtown makeover. Saving North

Creek Forest would complement this effort by assuring access to quality green spaces and natural habitat within its city boundaries. If Bothell responds favorably to this opportunity, it will indeed be a *great* place to live.

Good Happens

Waterway 18 Park after its make-over
© Woody Wheeler

One small section of abused and neglected shoreline along Seattle's Lake Union has recently been restored into a beautiful waterfront green space. The site is Waterway 18 or Northlake Beach, just east of Gas Works Park. Restoring it was a quadruple-win for Seattle. How? The people won, the fish won, habitat won, and the Wallingford/Fremont neighborhoods won. It took about five years to make this happen, which is lightning fast for Seattle.

When I first started working on this project for the Seattle Parks Foundation, Waterway 18 was not a friendly place. Among other things, it was afflicted by drug dealers, garbage dumping, invasive plants, fish-hostile rip-rap walls, rocky rubble strewn about, and a threadbare appearance. Now when you look up at this site, you will notice that it has been completely transformed from a place for crime to a public park complete with native plant landscaping, a well-defined area for small boat launches, and a staging/teaching area for boating classes.

As the Seattle Parks Foundation website says, "The project enhanced the waterway's natural and recreational assets, protecting the beach for native plants, lake access, and salmon." Like many projects of this kind, this one was a partnership between multiple entities, including The Seattle Parks Foundation, Washington Department of Natural Resources, Seattle Departments of Neighborhoods and Transportation, the Sea Scouts, and Outrigger Canoe Club. Good can and does happen.

Keep the Green Fire Burning

The year 1969 was an exciting, and tumultuous time in U.S. history. We were enmeshed in an unpopular war. Demonstrations raged about peace, civil and women's rights, and the environment. The Woodstock Music Festival celebrated the musical explosion that mirrored the social and political explosions of the Sixties.

Meanwhile on the far Northwestern coast in the mellow college town of Bellingham, Washington, one of the first Environmental Studies Programs in the U.S. was born. Huxley College, a new cluster campus of Western Washington University, was established to host this program. Its namesake, Thomas Henry Huxley, vigorously defended Charles Darwin's theory of evolution more than two centuries ago.

The story of Huxley College was chronicled in *Green Fire*, written by author and Huxley assistant professor of environmental journalism Bill Dietrich. *Green Fire* refers to the passion for the environment exhibited by Huxley students, faculty, and graduates. Although *Green Fire* is about Huxley, it is also emblematic of a worldwide passion for environmental stewardship that has grown exponentially in the past four decades.

When Huxley College first offered Environmental Studies, it was one of very few colleges to do so. Middlebury, Williams, and University of California, Berkeley were the others. Today, according to the College Board, 416 colleges in the U.S. offer Environmental Studies programs. This is how the College Board described this major, "Students of environmental studies use what they learn in the sciences, social sciences, and humanities to understand environmental problems. They look at how we interact with the natural world and come up with ideas for how we can prevent its destruction."

Green Fire author Bill Dietrich summarized Huxley's strengths well: "What it [Huxley College] does have is a consistent mission, to produce environmental problem solvers, and a quiet, persistent, unquenchable fire in its belly to make the world a better, more sustainable place. And for forty years, that has been quite enough."

I was one of the relative few who majored in environmental studies at Huxley in the early 1970s. Back then, we did so purely to follow our passions. There were precious few environmental jobs or careers available. There are many more opportunities in this field now. Given the host and magnitude of environmental issues that we face, there should be.

Over the years, the science component of Environmental Studies has been strengthened, giving students a better foundation from which to grasp environmental issues. Prior to coming to Huxley, I had taken two years of science as a Wildlife Biology major at University of Montana, which served me well. Now, as stated in *Green Fire,* Huxley has significantly increased its emphasis on science course work.

It gives me hope that today more students are majoring in Environmental Studies. One of my daughters is among them. Environmental Studies is not just a good idea: it is essential to our survival. Our very lives and the health of Planet Earth depend upon it. We absolutely need to keep the green fire burning.

Chapter 5 - Traveling to Meet New Species

Burnham, Daley, and Ward

Iconic Prairie Coneflowers in front of downtown Chicago skyscrapers
© Heather Phillips

Millennium Park plantings soften Chicago's urban core
© Heather Phillips

No, this is not a law firm. It is an historic dream team, or green team, that made Chicago's waterfront the spectacular place that it is today. An architect, a mayor, and a businessman, these three all had vision and they were all doers. The result of their combined efforts, along with the efforts of many other key players (like landscape architect Frederick Law Olmsted) is spectacular:

- All but four miles of Chicago's twenty-eight-mile lakefront is now park land.
- There are thirty-three public beaches on Chicago's waterfront.
- An eighteen-mile lakefront bike/pedestrian trail runs along the city's waterfront.

Millennium Park, built on a lid over the Illinois Central railroad, connects downtown Chicago to Lake Michigan with a fascinating mosaic of public art works, native plant gardens, a performing art center, and a network of creatively designed bridges leading to Lake Michigan parks, beaches, and to the Art Institute.

How did these three visionary men help make all of this possible?

Daniel Burnham managed the 1893 World's Columbian Exhibition in Chicago, one of the greatest events in U.S. history, chronicled in the fascinating book *Devil in the White City* by Eric Larson. Burnham was not only a great architect, but a gifted facilitator and the co-author of the 1909 Burnham plan, which included the tenets that the lakefront by right belonged to the people and that everyone should live within walking distance of a park.

Richard Daley served as Mayor of Chicago for twenty-two years, and led the effort to "make Chicago the greenest city in the U.S." As he said, "...when you do such things as planting trees and creating open space, when you invest resources to remove pollution from the air and encourage the construction of buildings that are smart for the environment, then you enhance quality of life for all the residents of the city."

To support his rhetoric, Daley took bold action. He closed down a small private airport and converted it to a native prairie, and he led the public/private partnership that resulted in Millennium Park, the crown jewel of the Chicago waterfront park system. Daley also had 600,000 trees planted, 85 miles of landscaped medians installed, and 600 roof gardens built, including a 20,000 square foot garden atop City Hall. The city is much greener because of him.

Aaron Montgomery Ward founded the nation's first mail order catalog in 1872, which led to the creation of the Montgomery Ward department stores. Not simply content with counting his money, or fighting off taxation and regulations, Ward cared (the operative word) for others and the welfare of his city. He wanted poor people to have access to Chicago's waterfront. In his words, the Chicago lakefront must be "forever open, clean, and free." Toward this end, he sued the city of Chicago twice to force it to remove buildings and structures from the lakefront and to prevent it from building new ones. Ward led the fight that started back in the 1930s to transform the city waterfront from a rail yard to a vast network of lakefront parklands. He had the imagination and vision to realize that this was possible. He looked up and visualized a better place. Chicago now has a spectacular lakefront because his vision was realized.

Burnham, Daley, and Ward's vision is alive and beautiful today. Chicagoans and visitors flock to the lakefront by the millions to access the lake, its beaches, free art exhibits, and concerts. So many more cities could learn from this fine example of what Chicago author Julia Sniderman Bachrach refers to as "A City in a Garden."

Resplendent Costa Rica

Costa Rican Resplendent Quetzal

"Resplendent" usually refers to Costa Rica's iconic bird, the Resplendent Quetzal. It could also refer to the entire country, which lives up to the term that means "shining, dazzling" and "brilliant."

Although often seen in Costa Rica, the Resplendent Quetzal is Guatemala's national bird. The name "Quetzal" derives from the Aztec word "quetzalli" for things that are precious or beautiful. Only Aztec royalty were allowed to wear Quetzal plumes.

Recently, I had the good fortune to host a Naturalist Journey to Costa Rica. There, because we frequently looked up, we saw 230 species of birds, along with a myriad of varieties of flora and fauna, ranging from Howler Monkeys to Green Iguanas, Basilisk Lizards, Caiman, White-collared Peccaries, and butterflies. We saw Quetzals too—a total of six—in two different locations. It was my first time to see this magnificent bird. No amount of photos, videos, or descriptions can prepare you for the sight of these birds in their native habitat. Seeing a Quetzal is an awe-inspiring experience!

The most ornate members of the Trogon family, Resplendent Quetzals inhabit tropical rainforests and nest in holes they drill in soft, decaying tree snags. Their diet comprises 80 percent wild avocados, with the balance made up by lizards and insects. According to *National Geographic*, the population of Quetzals is threatened throughout most of its range, except in Costa Rica: "In some areas, most notably Costa Rica's cloud forests, protected lands preserve habitat for the birds and provide opportunities for eco-tourists and eager bird watchers from around the globe."

Costa Rica's conservation efforts are indeed impressive:

- Twenty-five percent of the country, roughly two times the size of the state of Vermont, is protected for its habitat values.
- A national organization inventories its biota: The National Biodiversity Institute.

- Costa Rica ranked first among the Americas in a 2012 Environmental Performance Index.
- Costa Rica ranks as the greenest country in the world according to the New Economics Foundation.

May we all learn from Costa Rica's example. In the meantime, have a Quetzalli day!

Wallula Gap—Legendary Landscape

A soft autumn glow illuminated a vast expanse of the Columbia River canyon as we pulled off the highway into a small gravel parking area in southeastern Washington between the Tri-Cities and Walla Walla, Washington. It would be easy to miss this place if you did not look up. Two Red-tailed Hawks soared along the sage and juniper-encrusted ridgeline, welcoming us to this enchanting place. A Prairie Falcon streaked by, stirring up a flock of Juncos. We crossed through a break in the barbed wire fence and hiked the quarter-mile trail through Sagebrush and Rabbit Brush to the captivating double basalt columns looming above, known as the Twin Sisters.

A sign near the Twin Sisters contains the following legend, "The large basalt pillars in front of you are actually two Cayuse Indian sisters ... for many years Coyote lived happily with the sisters, but after a while he became jealous of them. Using his supernatural powers, coyote changed two of his wives into basalt pillars."

More than twelve thousand years ago, pre-people, a series of massive floods churned through Wallula Gap. According to Don Snow, Senior Lecturer of Environmental Studies at Whitman College, "Wallula Gap had formed a temporary hydraulic dam, partially stopping the largest floods the planet has ever seen from the super-fast flow that drained glacial Lake Missoula hundreds of miles away."

These floods occurred multiple times. They filled Wallula Gap up over a thousand feet deep, not only with water, but also with giant icebergs, often serving as rafts for huge boulders that were later deposited as glacial erratics. The currents were estimated to be between forty and fifty miles per hour. It is hard to imagine floods of this scale, but their evidence is imprinted on the landscape.

"Wallula" means a place where a small stream runs into a larger one: in this case where the Walla Walla River meets the Columbia River. Once a thriving trading post, Fort Walla Walla was located here. The nearby town of Wallula was once a major hub of rail and shipping commerce. Today, it is a sleepy two-hundred-person town.

This is a spectacular landscape with a spectacular story. Who knew? Thanks to a recent book, *Where the Great River Bends—A Natural and Human History of the Columbia at Wallula* edited by Robert J. Carson, a Whitman College geology professor, more people are discovering it. Carson continues to bring scores of students to the Gap to study its geologic and other natural wonders.

Currently, Wallula Gap is one of seventeen National Natural Landmarks in the state of Washington. It will likely become part of the new Ice Age Floods National Geologic Trail. Whitman College recently established a biological field station nearby. But the site also suffers from vandalism and graffiti. As Carson writes in his book, "Graffiti on the Twin Sisters is a problem; more visitor use, including rock climbing, would decrease vandalism."

Could Wallula Gap be a candidate for a National Monument? It is definitely worthy.

Shake and Shriek

Following the massive earthquake that struck Chile in 2010, there were daily aftershocks for some time. We felt four of them during our stay in the Valparaiso area three weeks after the big quake. One particularly strong aftershock triggered an interesting reaction from some local avian residents.

At 4:35 AM, on March 27, I awoke to creaking and shaking in our Vina del Mar hotel room. It was a 5.3 quake that lasted thirty seconds. Immediately afterward, I heard the raucous shrieking of Kelp Gulls who did not like having their perches shaken. Then I looked up at them through our hotel window and saw them calling from their rooftop perches. Kelp Gulls are common in central and southern Chile. They often hang out in groups and are described in *Birds of Southern South America* as being "rowdy" and having an "onomatopoetic" call. According to Webster's the word "onomatopoetic" refers to a voice "imitating the natural sound associated with the object or action involved; echoism." This was the first time I had ever heard bird vocalizations prompted by an earthquake. It has been suggested that birds and animals might have the ability to detect low frequency sounds such as those emitted by an earthquake. The gulls perched on buildings would certainly be able to detect vibrations through their feet.

Charles Darwin wrote of his 1835 visit to earthquake-ravaged Concepcion, Chile in Voyage of the Beagle , "A bad earthquake at once destroys our oldest associations: the earth, the very emblem of solidity, has moved beneath our feet like a thin crust over a fluid." This apparently is as true for gulls as it is for us.

A Mag(ellanic) Experience

Magellanic Penguin with nesting material
© Kyle and Melanie Elliot

Each year, some 150,000 Magellanic Penguins nest on Magdalena Island in the Straits of Magellan off the southern tip of South America. To see them, my family and I took a covered zodiac on a rough ten-mile crossing to the small windblown island. Thanks to Dramamine and piped-in Beatles tunes, we arrived at Magdalena Island in good health and spirits.

Once there, temperatures were just above freezing with steadily falling sleet. We put on so many layers that we looked and walked like the penguins ourselves. We hiked the short, cordoned-off trail designed to minimize disturbance to the penguins. Signs instructed us to remain on the trails. The penguins, however, were not shy about going anywhere on the island, including on the trails just feet away from us.

Magellanic Penguins are one of eighteen species of penguins throughout the world. Native to South America, they breed in coastal Argentina, Chile, and the Falkland Islands. They are seafood specialists, dining on a variety of fish including anchovies, sardines, hake, and cod. Among their many predators are Orcas, Fur Seals, Sea Lions, foxes, rats, domestic cats, and birds including Fulmars, Skuas, and various gulls, which primarily prey upon the young.

The island resembled Swiss cheese with its numerous penguin burrows. Hundreds of penguins were visible and audible everywhere. They walked in purposeful-looking groups, stood guard by their burrows, and brayed like donkeys or let loose with their rhythmic "ha-ha-ha" call with their head pointed skyward. It was absolutely captivating.

Our experience put a face on a species that is threatened by oil spills and climate change. The latter is forcing the birds to swim farther to find food according to researchers at the University of Washington. Magellanic Penguin chicks that already had to contend with predation and starvation now have to deal with more intense and rainy storms as well as hot weather. Combined, these factors are taking a toll on their population.

According to University of Washington scientist and lead author of the study, Dee Boersma, "Rainfall is killing a lot of penguins, and so is heat, and those are two new causes." Protecting the penguins equals protecting ourselves by preventing oil spills and addressing climate change. We can make a difference here and elsewhere, if we want to. Here's hoping we do. Our collective futures depend upon it.

The Ultimate Christmas Gift

In 2005, we received the ultimate Christmas gift.

My family and I were in Jaco, Costa Rica, a funky beach, surfing, fishing, and tourist town on the Pacific Coast. We were on the last leg of a wonderful tour of the country that included rain forests, beaches, volcanoes, rivers, wetlands, as well as cultural sites such as a banana processing plant, a green coffee plantation, and museums in San Jose.

Early on Christmas morning, we were staying in a hotel in Jaco that overlooked the distant Pacific. My wife called me urgently to the balcony where she had looked up and spotted several remarkable birds in flight. Together we watched in astonishment as a group of half a dozen gaudy red, blue, and yellow Scarlet Macaws flew directly overhead, squawking loudly as they passed over the hotel rooftop. We were in a happy state of shock.

Later that morning during an outdoor breakfast, we saw and heard several more Macaw groups flying by. We pointed them out to the delight of other tour members. This was the first time that any of us had seen these remarkable and previously endangered birds in the wild.

The Scarlet Macaw is a strikingly beautiful representative of the parrot family that prefers rainforest habitat ranging from southern Mexico through Central America, up to the northern portion of South America. They are sexually dimorphic meaning that males and females look alike—both flat-out gorgeous! Due to hunting, poaching, and habitat destruction through deforestation as well as pesticide use by banana companies, Scarlet Macaw populations plummeted in the 1960s. They seem to have stabilized according to the World Conservation Union, which rated them a species of "Least Concern" in 2004.

This is hopeful news for the planet and for people who seek the ultimate gift.

Iberá—Wet Wonder of the World

Cattle Tyrant takes a ride on Capybara – Ibera Wetlands, Argentina
© Kyle and Melanie Elliot

Yacare Caiman – Ibera Wetlands, Argentina
© Kyle and Melanie Elliot

"Y bera" means "shining waters" in the indigenous Guaraní language, hence the name "Iberá." These shining waters form the second-largest complex of wetlands on earth after Brazil's Pantanal. Located in the Province of Corrientes in Northeast Argentina, relatively close to the cities of Posadas and Mercedes, this mix of swamps, bogs, stagnant lakes, natural sloughs, and watercourses comprise a natural area of astounding proportions.

The Iberá Wetlands encompass a five thousand square mile area drained by the Corrientes River, which flows into the Parana River. The Parana later empties into Rio de La Plata and the Atlantic Ocean at Buenos Aires' harbor. Prior to 2000, this wet natural wonder was only partially protected. Then a U.S. conservation-minded couple took action. Their story is as large-scale and spectacular as the area itself. And like any major conservation action, it was not without controversy.

Kristine and Douglas Tompkins are the Iberá Wetlands' primary conservation benefactors. Douglas Tompkins is the founder of North Face and Esprit clothing lines. Between 2000 and 2006, the Tompkins purchased more than 400,000 acres in Iberá Wetlands. They bought these properties then donated them to the Province of Corrientes with a guarantee that they would become a part of the Provincial Nature Reserve, and eventually a National Park. The Reserve itself was designated as such by the Province of Corrientes in 1983. It is currently a mix of private lands with productive activities that are compatible with conservation activities and public lands in reserve status—the latter purchased and protected mostly by the Tompkins and their organization, The Conservation Land Trust. Their goal is to continue protecting lands in the core of the reserve, ultimately leading to its being designated an Argentinean National Park.

What prompted the Tompkins to make such huge and generous contributions to conservation in Argentina? In their words,

"Some people have speculated wildly about our motivations. First and foremost we believe that wilderness areas and wildlife have an intrinsic value and the creatures at home in them have a right to exist for their own sakes. Every human being should care about the diversity of life, the myriad species that are our fellow members of the land community, and be willing to take action, at whatever level necessary to see that there is enough secure habitat for all species to flourish."

Regarding species, an incredible diversity of them exists in Iberá Wetlands. There are 360 species on Iberá Wetlands' bird list. To put this into perspective, during our four-day visit, we saw 207 species of birds, including 107 in one day. This kind of bird abundance and diversity does not exist everywhere. Our bird lists included numerous life birds, such as Jabiru, Dusty-legged Guan, multiple Seedeaters, Spinetails, three species of Cardinals, and one species of Tyrant with an especially impressive name: Pearly-vented Tody Tyrant. In addition, Iberá Reserve hosts hundreds of Capybara, the world's largest rodent, which resembles a Beaver crossed with a large rat; Marsh Deer, Howler Monkeys, Maned Wolves, Crab-eating Foxes, more Caiman than you can shake a stick at, 125 species of fish, 63 reptiles including Yellow Anaconda, and 40 species of amphibians.

Accessing this extraordinary place is not easy. The closest major airport is in Posada—four hours away; there is no train station, no port, no paved roads, and only one very small, sleepy town: Colonia Pellegrini. We met our driver, Alejandro, in Posada in the late afternoon to begin the seventy-five-mile journey to Iberá—most of it by dirt roads. He was an excellent bird and wildlife spotter, which was remarkable, because he did so at dusk without binoculars while navigating a truck along a rough dirt road. Alejandro was always looking up; he was incredibly observant. Just before nightfall, he found a Savanna Hawk, an Aplomado Falcon, and our first Capybara.

After the marathon three-hour dirt road trip, we arrived at our simple but nice lodge in complete darkness. A loud chorus of frogs and crickets greeted us; the dense humid air was literally vibrating with unseen life forms.

In the morning we awoke to a magical scene including extensive wetlands with board walks in the foreground and a large lagoon beyond. At the edge of the hotel deck, Giant Wood Rails and Southern Lapwings scurried about protecting their respective territories, nests, and young. Two huge Southern Screamers flew in and landed in a wet (everything is wet here) patch of grass. The entire area did shine as the Guarani noted in their naming of Ibera as a place of shining waters. Beneath its pale blue humid sky with puffy clouds, it was reminiscent of the Midwestern U.S. skies that I recalled seeing as a kid.

Later that day we met our guide, Jose, and a Canadian couple who were expert birders, for a sensational boat tour of the lagoon. Jose was a former gaucho, now employed as a nature tour guide and hotel grounds maintenance staff person. Like all of our Argentine guides, he had no scope, camera, or binoculars, just incredibly keen senses and an impressive knowledge of the flora and fauna.

While skimming across the shallow lagoon, we noticed the extensive, dense mats of aquatic vegetation, the likes of which we had never seen before. Water Hyacinths are abundant here as are "embalsados"—floating islands of vegetation. Along the shores are very few buildings, ranches, or other signs of civilization, save for one bridge across the lagoon and the power lines that cross it.

Soon we spotted our first-ever Large-billed Tern; a huge Caiman with its jaws propped open wide; and a herd of Capybara partially submerged in the aquatic vegetation with plants adorning their heads like gaudy green jewelry. Birds rode atop the Capybaras as they walked through the shallows. Cattle Tyrants mainly did this, but so did other species, including a Snowy Egret.

The large lagoon—one of two that are several miles wide and long—teems with birds and wildlife. In one small bay we saw two Marsh Deer, multiple Wattled Jacana, Brazilian Ducks, a White-throated Heron, nesting Thorn Birds, a Sooty Tyrannulet, Tawny-headed Swallows, and more. We literally did not know where to look and our heads were on constant swivels. We probably made our guide Jose dizzy with all of our simultaneous sightings and questions.

An unusually heavy, torrential downpour of a rainstorm settled in on our second night, continuing through the next day. All roads became impassable, and the power went out for twenty-four hours. We were marooned at the hotel and its network of elevated decks and board walks. The roads were the consistency of thick mud gumbo. They were virtually impassable to vehicles and made even walking difficult.

The view from our lodge deck was nonetheless impressive. Birds such as Red-crested Cardinals perched on the deck furniture on the covered deck to take refuge from the pouring rain; their crests looked as though the hair-stylist had used too much gel. Vermillion Flycatchers, Whistling Herons and Rufescent Tiger-Herons were clearly visible in surrounding trees, and our first Limpkin of the trip wandered by at close range, amid the Giant Wood Rails. Of course we also had the trilogy of Argentina's most common birds: Rufous Horneros (the national bird), Rufous-collared Sparrows, and the Great Kiskadee, which we saw in every part of Argentina we visited whether wet, dry, urban, or rural.

Iberá is not a highly developed resort area. Its local town, Colonia Pellegrini, is a tiny, sleepy agricultural town gradually transitioning to an eco-tourist economy. There are a half-dozen or so hotels sprinkled around the town on the edge of the lagoon, but it's mostly made up of simple shops, tiny sole-proprietor Empanada stands, and abundant sheep, horses, cows, dogs, cats, and chickens that wander the town's dirt roads. The animals far outnumber the people. Their waste is everywhere, making walking in your sandals or barefoot undesirable.

Some government officials, ranchers, and corporate leaders resented the fact that Iberá Wetlands had been purchased and was being protected by foreigners. Some disapprove of the regulations; others have a speculative interest in the immense aquifer that underlies the area. Just as we have experienced in the United States, there are always people who oppose the creation of large refuges and/or national parks. Grand Teton National Park in Wyoming, for example, was held up for decades until another conservation philanthropist, John Rockefeller, bought a huge portion of it and held it until the park finally gained political approval.

In the final analysis, Iberá is an incredible place of worldwide ecological significance and well worth saving. As Kristine and Douglas Tompkins say in their eloquent statement about saving this place and others in the Southern Cone of South America, "Paraphrasing the great conservationist David Brower and endorsing his sentiment, we believe that there will be no social justice, no economy, no art and culture, no democracy or gender equality—no human society at all—on a dead planet." Thanks to the Tompkins, the Conservation Land Trust and the Government of Argentina, Iberá Wetlands remain an extraordinary and vital wet wonder of the world.

Bird Airports

As you drive south from Vancouver, British Columbia, through its 2.4 million person metropolitan area, you pass by the airport. An hour further south, you come to another one, but this one serves only feathered aircraft. Located near suburban Ladner, British Columbia, this bustling international airport is called the George C. Reifel Migratory Bird Sanctuary.

To get there, you drive west of Ladner, then cross a narrow

wooden bridge over the south fork of the mighty Fraser River to Westham Island, situated in the mouth of the river, dividing the Fraser into northern and southern channels. Here you leave behind suburbia and re-enter the rich farmland that comprised much of this area before. In winter, you are likely to see Bald Eagles, Trumpeter Swans, and maybe a Peregrine Falcon along this stretch. Then, after a few kilometers of 90-degree turns that trace property boundaries, you turn onto the road into the George C. Reifel Migratory Bird Sanctuary.

The first time I visited the 850-acre/300 hectare George C. Reifel Sanctuary on British Columbia's Fraser River Delta in the late 1970s, I remarked to my college friends that it resembled a "bird airport." A plethora of waterfowl were taking off and landing in the many ponds and channels that comprise this sanctuary, making loud and frequent splashing sounds as they skidded to their watery landings all around us. Buffleheads, Canvasbacks, Teal, Scaup, Wigeon, and Mallards were among the thousands of ducks at this sanctuary. It was exhilarating to be surrounded by so many multicolored flying, swimming waterfowl.

Each winter, I revisit this marvelous place. Recently, my wife and I encountered a flock of more than eight-hundred Snow Geese as we drove into the sanctuary entrance, close enough to take movies complete with their constant chatter as a sound track. This flock was actively feeding in preparation for its journey back to its Wrangel Island, Russia breeding grounds. When we opened the door of our car in the refuge parking lot, three Sandhill Cranes flew overhead, just thirty feet above us, uttering their loud, resonant, rattling calls, a "prehistoric" sound that reminded us that birds are indeed descendents of dinosaurs.

Within thirty minutes of walking through this sanctuary we saw four Black-crowned Night Herons, a Merlin, several Bald Eagles, and an uncountable numbers of Gadwall, Wigeon,

Pintail, and Mallard ducks. You know you are in a good bird refuge when you don't know what to look at first, and, and where rare sightings occur along with the common. Our rarity was a female Northern Goshawk hunting in the Alder trees at the western edge of the sanctuary. We also enjoyed a rare look at a common species—the Great Blue Heron—in a flock of forty-five flying together above us, creating a blue-gray airborne spectacle. Neither of us had ever seen so many herons in flight together before. By the time we were done with our three-hour walk in 35-degree temperatures and snow flurries, we'd tallied fifty-one species of birds. More than 280 species have been recorded at Reifel Sanctuary over the years.

Bird airports like Reifel Sanctuary exist because of people like the Reifel family who had foresight and conservation values. George C. Reifel purchased the property on an island in the Fraser River Delta in 1927 to make it into a family retreat. It already had three natural sloughs that traversed the island at the mouth of British Columbia's largest river. He constructed dykes and causeways to create prime waterfowl habitat. Eventually, he granted a lease to the British Columbia Waterfowl Society and involved Ducks Unlimited in the management of his property.

Years later, the Reifel family negotiated a combined sale and donation to the Government of Canada, which agreed to manage the site for its waterfowl and to keep George Reifel's name. Located within an hour's drive from the city of Vancouver and close to the U.S. border, Reifel Sanctuary hosts more than 600,000 human visitors annually.

The sanctuary is strategically located at the mouth of the Fraser River, the largest estuary along the Pacific Coast of North America. Along with the larger, adjacent Alaksen National Wildlife Refuge, it is a crossroad for migratory birds that travel from twenty other countries and three continents. This is not just a bird airport; it is an international bird airport.

Among the many visitors are kids and families. Reifel

Sanctuary, with its flat trails, numerous feeders, and policy of selling bags of grain to feed the birds, is an attractive outing for kids, families, and tourists of all kinds. This is a great way to connect people to nature in a up-close and personal way. Kids can have a "wow!" nature experience that will help develop an appreciation for birds and nature. Here they can learn how to look up and notice the amazing living world that exists all around them. One child we once brought to this refuge years ago has since become an ornithologist. Another has become an environmental science major.

Thankfully, bird airports like Reifel Sanctuary exist throughout the U.S., Canada, and other parts of the world. Originally established as hunting preserves, these reserves now cater to people who hunt with cameras, binoculars, and their own two eyes. They provide strategic stopover, feeding, resting, and staging areas for birds migrating along their flyways.

Like parks and other nature preserves, Wildlife Refuges are testimony to the intelligence and compassion of the human species. They are a good investment because we rely upon the health of the planet as much as birds and other wildlife do. We also need inspiration and joy, which sanctuaries like Reifel provide in abundance.

An Affinity for Aesthetics

Harlequin Duck
© Jeff Larsen

If there were a bird beauty contest, the Harlequin Duck would be a serious contestant, if not a finalist. The name "harlequin" is derived from the comic entertainers in Europe who wore colorful, distinctively patterned costumes; thus the Latin name for this striking duck: "*Histrionicus histrionicus*."

Not only does this sea duck, especially the male, have exquisite plumage, but Harlequin Ducks live in exquisite surroundings. This is due to their habitat preference for fast-flowing waters.

Harlequin Ducks are one of the few waterfowl species that breed on forested mountain streams in the North Cascades, Northern Rocky and Selkirk Mountains in the West, and in the Laurentian Mountains in northeastern Canada. They spend winters on rocky shorelines battered by turbulent waves and strong tidal currents. In the spring and summer, you can find them in mountain streams in places like Glacier, the North Cascades, or the Olympic National Parks. During fall and winter, they inhabit places like the San Juan Islands, Gulf Islands, or coastal Maine, the latter of which provides territory for up to half of the eastern wintering population of Harlequin Ducks. These are very scenic places indeed, frequented by one of the most beautiful ducks found in nature.

Harlequin Ducks eat insects, fish, and marine invertebrates, often on or near the bottom of the sea or river. They are considered to be sea ducks due to their diving skills, salt-water, and cold-weather tolerance, and their preference for animal foods. The eastern population of Harlequin Duck is on the Canadian Endangered Species list and Harlequins are considered threatened in Maine. They are a "species of special concern" in the western United States. In their scenic natural environment, they are a sight to behold, if you bother to look up.

Snowy Irruption

Snowy Owl
© Jeff Larsen

Each winter, those of us who live in the northern United States and southern Canada are graced by the presence of majestic Snowy Owls. Every few years, the owls migrate south in significant numbers. When this happens across, a Snowy irruption is underway!

"Irruptions" are irregular migratory movements that depend upon such factors as food availability and/or a change in season. In the case of Snowy Owls, irruptions have a lot to do with the availability of their primary food source: lemmings. Previously, it was thought that Snowy Owls came south due to periodic crashes in the lemming population. It is now thought that Snowy Owls leave primarily after a big lemming year when a resultant bumper crop of young owls need food and new territory. These young owls tend to venture south.

Lemmings are small mouse-like rodents that remain active all year long; they do not hibernate. They eat shrubs, herbs, and sedges in summer, and willow buds, leaves, twigs, and bark during the winter months. The notion that lemmings commit mass suicide is a myth. They do, however, run as a group and will swim across lakes or streams to another land mass.

Snowy Owls are one of the few resident bird species of the Arctic tundra. The others are Gyrfalcon, Willow and Rock Ptarmigans, and the Common Raven. Even though there are relatively few bird species in the Arctic, predators still exist. Snowy Owls vigorously defend their nesting territories from wolves and Arctic Foxes. Other breeding birds like Snow Geese, Brant, and Common Eiders will sometimes nest near Snowy Owls to reduce attacks from Arctic Foxes.

Snowy Owls perch in open areas waiting for their prey, which often consists of voles, other rodents, and/or birds. A recent wintering owl that stopped by briefly in a Seattle park killed and ate a gull. Their white color makes them conspicuous in our blue-green-gray winter landscape. In their Arctic home, however, white provides the perfect camouflage against the snow.

If you want to see a Snowy Owl, check your local birding sightings, which are now often posted online. Look for the owls calmly sitting atop trees, power poles, driftwood, snags, small hills, rooftops, or any perch that provides a view of open country. We are so accustomed to seeing garbage around that we sometimes fail to investigate large white items in the countryside, assuming that we're seeing nothing more than a discarded plastic gallon jug. Check these "objects" out with binoculars; a few might just be Snowy Owls instead.

Chapter 6 - The Nature of Politics

Celebrate Science

Today my wife can return to work thanks to cold medicine. I just led a birding and natural history field trip in a former landfill that the University of Washington has since restored into a diverse natural area. My father-in-law is receiving a colonoscopy to assess his health status. One of my daughters flew to Washington, DC to visit him in a jet aircraft, and tonight, my wife and I will eat in a smoke-free restaurant. I thank scientists for making all of these things possible.

There are some who discount science and scientists. Long ago, we called these science disbelievers members of the Flat Earth Society. Today, some politicians could be characterized as anti-science, modern-day Flat Earth Society members who deny climate change, evolution, and any form of environmental destruction. These bold deceivers prefer not to let science or facts get in the way. Let's not go there. Science is a big reason why we can enjoy living here—in a technologically-advanced, first-world, democratic nation.

What has science done for you lately? How about medicine, agriculture, all forms of transportation and energy, clean water and sewage treatment, and weather forecasting, just to name a few of the many ways that science has improved our lives. Historically, we have been good at science, have embraced it, and it has served us well. Lately, however, due to well-financed, highly visible disinformation campaigns, doubt has been heaped upon legitimate science.

Scientists have a thorough process of vetting their discoveries and opinions to make sure they are valid, and we as a society benefit from the scientific consensus they arrive at. Scientists develop hypotheses and test them; they are skeptical by training. Their theories do not gain acceptance until they have been

115

subjected to rigorous peer review and can be validated by factual evidence based on extensive research and data.

Here is one example of applied science that we can all relate to: antibiotics. When you take an antibiotic it kills bacterial infections in your system. These are truly wonder drugs that have saved untold numbers of lives and spared millions from disease-related misery. Scientists created antibiotics and most other medicinal drugs.

Science also helps us understand why we must take antibiotics until the prescription is finished. Evolution is at play here. If you stop taking antibiotics mid-cycle (don't try this at home), a few surviving antibiotic-resistant bacteria will survive and reproduce, become many, and continue infecting your body. In short, you have helped the bacteria evolve to tolerate a partial dose of the antibiotic. Maybe people who don't believe in science or evolution should stop taking antibiotics.

To discredit science would be equally ignorant and self-destructive. But we have seen this form of public disservice before as recalled by Al Gore in his recent article "Climate of Denial" (www.rollingstone.com). "A half-century ago, when science and reason established the linkage between cigarettes and lung diseases, the tobacco industry hired actors, dressed them up as doctors, and paid them to look into television cameras and tell people that the linkage revealed in the Surgeon General's Report was not real at all. The show went on for decades, with more Americans killed each year by cigarettes than all of the U.S. soldiers killed in all of World War II."

Gore also wrote about the continual challenge to gain acceptance for climate change despite overwhelming evidence supporting it: "The scientific consensus is far stronger today than at any time in the past. Here is the truth: The Earth is round; Saddam Hussein did not attack us on 9/11; Elvis is dead; Obama was born in the United States; and the climate crisis is real. It is time to act."

Let's apply our most intelligent and time-tested methods to

addressing the world's problems through science. Doing so, we have a chance of saving ourselves and planet Earth.

Return of the Lorax

The late great Theodor Seuss Geisel—aka Dr. Seuss—was ahead of his time. While his books delight, they also educate kids and their parents about vital issues ranging from racial inequality to environmental destruction. Some of his books are cautionary tales.

An animated film version of one of these, *The Lorax*, was released in 2012. Based upon Dr. Seuss's 1971 book, it features a faceless, greedy industrialist, "the Once-ler" (not exactly a sustainable name), who exploits resources rapaciously, causing major environmental damage as he manufactures "Thneeds." These are shapeless sweater sorts of items that, as he put it "everyone needs." The Lorax, a wizened advocate who "speaks for the trees, because the trees have no tongues," confronts the Once-ler about the environmental impacts of his business. A fascinating, yet realistic dialogue ensues.

The Lorax represents a voice of environmental consciousness that we once again need to hear. We humans struggle mightily to understand our place in nature. At times we seem to grasp it, as illustrated by the green movement, recycling, sustainable development, and fuel-efficient cars. But then we backslide, as evidenced by climate change denial, the anti-science, and anti-evolution crowd. It is hard for us to accept our responsibilities as earth stewards.

The film version of *The Lorax* provides hope. We all know the power that media holds to transform and inspire. The challenge is to change our culture so that damaging the environment becomes socially unacceptable, just as smoking in public places or throwing trash out the window of your car has become socially unacceptable. Perhaps the film retelling of

The Lorax is one step toward this change. The environmental messages contained in it bear repeating, and nobody could say them in a more creative, compelling way than Dr. Seuss. To wit, "Unless someone like you cares a whole awful lot, nothing is going to get better, it's not."

Welcome back and stay around indefinitely, Lorax; we need you to remind us to look up and steward the earth!

Bipartisan Conservation

Conservation should be a bipartisan issue with widespread public support. It used to be. A recent candidate who squarely addressed it was Jon Huntsman. He correctly asserted that "Conservation is conservative."

Conservation means the wise use of natural resources. These resources are the savings account, so to speak, that our planet provides for future generations, but only if we use those resources wisely. In the past, politicians of both major U.S. political parties as well as independents supported conservation efforts.

- **Teddy Roosevelt**, Republican president, later independent (Bull Moose Party), established National Forests, National Wildlife Refuges, and added to our National Park system.
- **Franklin Delano Roosevelt**, Democratic president, created the Civilian Conservation Corps, which helped build numerous National Park facilities, and helped finalize new National Parks, including Grand Teton and Olympic.
- **Dwight Eisenhower**, Republican president, donated his family farm to the National Park Service.
- **Richard Nixon**, Republican president, signed into law the *Clean Air Act*, the *Clean Water Act*, and the *Endangered Species Act*, and launched the Environmental Protection Agency.

- **Jimmy Carter,** Democratic president, established the Wild and Scenic River designation through the *Wild and Scenic River Act*, and protected huge areas of Alaskan wilderness. He also asked us to conserve energy (we did not listen very well).
- **Bill Clinton**, Democratic president, added seventeen new National Monuments, increased protection for wetlands and old-growth forests, and banned road building in sixty million acres of wilderness areas in National Forests.

Looking after our natural assets should be a source of pride and patriotism—for all parties concerned. When we look up, we should be proud of the way our respective countries manage their natural resources.

Have We Evolved?

While visiting snowy Washington D.C., my daughter and I took in a Charles Darwin exhibit at the Smithsonian. As we strolled through, I wondered if we humans have evolved—not in a physical way but rather in our treatment of one another and the planet.

Here are two accomplishments in the last fifty years that suggest we have:

Civil Rights: Another Smithsonian exhibit featured a replica of the Greensboro, North Carolina lunch counter where, fifty years ago, four brave African American college students refused to leave, defying the former discriminatory practices of this and many other businesses and institutions. Today, an African American president and his family reside less than a mile from this exhibit in the White House, and Washington DC has its fifth African American mayor.

Bald Eagle Conservation: Soon after arriving in DC, I spotted a Bald Eagle soaring over the Potomac River. Back in the early

1960s, the Bald Eagle population in the U.S. had plummeted to only 417 pairs in the lower forty-eight states. Now more than 7,000 pairs inhabit the continental U.S., including 850 pairs in Washington State alone! Bald Eagles are no longer on the Endangered Species list. This happened thanks to a combination of the banning of DDT, the *Endangered Species Act*, and vigorous protection of Bald Eagle nesting sites.

I realize there have also been transgressions in the past fifty years, and areas of no progress. But consider other major positive changes that have occurred since then, such as no-smoking laws, recycling, women's rights, gay rights, and the end of South African Apartheid, just to name a few. We can evolve if we want to.

Embracing Vulture and Sparrow Culture

Turkey Vultures soaring
© Kyle and Melanie Elliot

Sometimes when people don't understand or appreciate living things, they want to destroy them. Often they do this without knowledge of the species' value to the environment. Consider vultures and sparrows.

Vultures are ugly. They eat dead things and they roost in groups that resemble scary Halloween displays. They look menacing, but looks can be deceiving.

Vultures are valuable scavengers that collectively form a global natural sanitation crew. By consuming dead animals, they keep the environment clean. If the millions (billions?) of carcasses around the world were left to rot and fester, we would have far more serious disease problems than we do to-day. Vultures prevent the spread of dangerous diseases such as rabies and anthrax by consuming the carcasses themselves, and by leading other wild animals to them, so the cleanup occurs quickly.

The ugly head of vultures is actually a smart adaptation to their lifestyle. Their naked heads remain cleaner than they would if they were covered with feathers. That bald head is perfect for feeding inside carcasses. It's similar to rubber gloves worn by doctors for sanitation purposes.

Through a combination of an excellent sense of smell and keen eyesight, vultures find and clean up carcasses all over the earth. According to the Cornell Lab of Ornithology, "The Turkey Vulture's heightened ability to detect odors—it can de-tect just a few parts per trillion —allows it to find dead animals (even) below a forest canopy."

Once vultures find dead animals, they not only consume them, but they sanitize them so they are not a disease threat. How? Ornithologist Van Harris wrote about this in his excellent 2012 column in the *Memphis Commercial Appeal* article, "*Vultures are Scary but Beneficial to Environment.*" What vultures do for us is actually a fabulous free service. We should be grateful! "In fact, the digestive juices of vultures are so powerful that most bacteria and viruses are killed before they pass out of the birds' digestive tracts. Vultures actually help control diseases in the environment by consuming animals that die of those diseases. Fortunately, Black and Turkey Vultures are now protected by law and allowed to help keep the countryside clean."

Sparrows, to the unaware, are drab, common, unimportant, and unremarkable. China's former dictator, Chairman Mao Zedong, certainly did not care for them. According to John Platt, a writer about endangered species for *Scientific American*: "One of Mao Zedong's first actions after collectivizing agriculture was intended to protect the farms. Sparrows, he was told, ate a lot of grain seeds, so Zedong ordered the people to go forth and kill all the sparrows. During the Great Sparrow Campaign, as it has been called, hundreds of millions of sparrows were killed....

The problem with the Great Sparrow Campaign became evident in 1960. The sparrows, it seemed, didn't only eat grain seeds. They also ate insects. With no birds to control them, insect populations boomed. Locusts, in particular swarmed over the country, eating everything they could find—including crops intended for human food. People on the other hand, quickly ran out of things to eat, and millions starved. Numbers vary, of course, with the official number from the Chinese government placed at 15 million.

One of the hardest things for humans to grasp is ecology: the interrelationship between living things and the environment. Part of the problem is that we are so busy looking downward and inward, that we sometimes become oblivious to it. Animals and all species are here for a reason. They have important niches and belong to this planet as much as we do. In the words of William Kittredge in his powerful autobiography *Hole in the Sky*, "We must define a story which encourages us to make use of the place where we live without killing it, and we must understand that the living world cannot be replicated."

Rocky Road to Wolf Recovery

Few species elicit such a mixture of love and ire as the Gray Wolf. In recent history, the Gray Wolf was eliminated from the Northern Rockies. In 1995-96, the fate of the wolves was reversed by the reintroduction of thirty-one wolves from Canada and the northern U.S. into Yellowstone Park, and thirty-five into the Frank Church River of No Return Wilderness in Idaho. As of 2013, nearly seventeen hundred Gray Wolves lived in the Greater Yellowstone Ecosystem (GYE), which encompasses Yellowstone and Grand Teton National Parks, seven National Forests and three National Wildlife Refuges—almost twenty million acres of contiguous public lands.

Far from celebrating the recovery of Gray Wolves, the three states surrounding the GYE—Montana, Wyoming, and Idaho—managed to delist wolves in 2011 from their former endangered status. In addition, they have reinstituted hunting and trapping that have so far resulted in the killing of eleven hundred wolves in their respective states. You might call this backlash, backsliding, or just plain backward. It has elements of all three.

When one of my participants from the U.K. on a Naturalist Journeys tour of Yellowstone Park heard about this, he was incredulous. Why would the U.S. invest in wolf recovery aided by the *Endangered Species Act* and public opinion only to have the entire effort sabotaged by a few rogue states through delisting and hunting? It is a good question.

Two tour groups I guided in the summer of 2013 had the pleasure of seeing wolves in Yellowstone National Park. It was pure magic as we watched a small pack of four wolves alternately resting, then splashing across the Yellowstone River to first hunt a Bison calf and later a juvenile elk (both hunts were unsuccessful), prior to cooling off and drinking in the river. This slice of wolf life took place in the Hayden Valley, enchanting at least a hundred onlookers for a solid hour. For some, including all in our group, this was the highlight of their trip.

None of us should take this experience for granted, nor should future wolf-watchers. As Kathy Lynch wrote in *The Wildlife News* article "Yellowstone Still the Best Place for Watching Wolves despite Many Killed in Hunt": "With only around 70 wolves in Yellowstone National Park, watchers hoping to see a wolf in the wild must be very patient and also very lucky." Apparently, we were both.

Tourism, like the kind my groups engage in, is big business for the three states that opted to shoot and delist wolves. Consider these statements from each of the three states websites in 2013:

> "Tourism is Montana's fastest-growing industry, supporting 37,000 jobs and 7% of the total state workforce."
> "The mineral extraction industry and the travel and tourism sector are the main drivers behind Wyoming's economy."
> "Tourism is the #5 industry in Idaho, employing 47,000 people and accounting for 7% of its workforce."

Yellowstone and Grand Teton Park draw four million tourists per year. Seeing wolves and other wildlife in these parks is a tremendous draw. One wonders where the disconnect is in the wolf policies of these three states. Isn't shooting wolves the equivalent of shooting themselves in the collective foot of their respective state economies?

Beyond tourism, wolves provide significant ecological values. These were brought into sharper focus by researchers from Oregon State University and Washington State University. They discovered that Yellowstone grizzlies consume more berries now that shrubs are starting to recover from elk over browsing. This recovery has occurred since the reintroduction of wolves, which reduced the elk herds. The vegetative recovery extends to other species as well. Removing wolves from Yellowstone Park in the early 1980s resulted in increased browsing by elk herds that led to the demise of young aspen and willow trees, shrubs, and tall herbaceous plants. These trees and plants have since recovered, providing food and shelter for a wide variety of animals and birds. Wolves are part of this story of vegetative recovery.

The entire GYE is richer and more diverse with wolves in it. But what about the elk, you might ask? They are still numerous: 3,915 elk were counted in Yellowstone Park in the winter of 2013 according the *Billings Gazette*, down 6 percent from last year's 4,174 count. This puts the Northern Elk herd that spends summers in Yellowstone and winters in Montana squarely within the 3,000-5,000 member range, Montana Fish Wildlife and Parks Department's objective for a sustainable population.

Shooting wolves also has the obvious negative effect upon wolf family structure and packs. According to Michael Robinson of the Center for Biodiversity, "Hunting wolves disrupts family bands, can leave pups to starve, and contributes to the dangerous genetic isolation of wolves in Yellowstone." One of the packs we normally see on my tours in Slough Creek, Yellowstone National Park, has dissolved after its alpha male was fatally shot outside the park in Wyoming's newly legalized hunt.

There is another side of this story. Wolves do predate on significant numbers of livestock—especially sheep. Not coincidentally, the three states—Montana, Wyoming, and Idaho— with the largest numbers of wolf predations, are the same states that have delisted Gray Wolves and legalized wolf hunts. The wolf-killed livestock numbers, however, are still small when compared to other causes of livestock fatalities. Carter Niemeyer, a former trapper and predator control agent in Montana puts wolf predation into perspective in his fascinating and insightful memoir *Wolfer*: "It is a fact that wolves kill so few livestock that the predators barely register on the pie chart of the U.S. Department of Agriculture's National Agriculture Statistics Service. It's respiratory and digestive diseases, birthing problems, old age, poisonous plants, and weather that cause most livestock deaths, although Coyotes can be hell on sheep." Niemeyer should know, because in his words, "Between 1987 and 2000 I skinned every animal in Montana that the wolves were accused of killing."

Nonetheless, Defenders of Wildlife, one of the leading wolf advocacy nonprofits, has acknowledged wolf predation and has raised more than one million dollars in payments over the past decade to compensate farmers and ranchers for wolf predation of their livestock. Defenders only provide compensation when wolf predation is the actual versus the supposed cause of mortality. It used to be Niemeyer's job to determine this.

Wolf management is not a simple issue. There are legitimate claims on both sides. There is also hyperbole and misinformation, sometimes disseminated by high-profile people. The current Governor of Idaho has implied that wolves are a direct threat to humans. This is not supported by any factual or scientific information. As Jim and Jamie Dutcher of *Living with Wolves* write, "Since wolves were re-introduced in 1995, not one violent encounter between wolves and human beings has taken place anywhere in the lower 48 states."

As we attempt to achieve responsible wolf management, let's allow science and facts to inform the debate instead of fairy tales and rural legends. Second, let's work with all parties involved, including environmentalists, and ranchers and farmers who suffer livestock predation, and find ways to compensate them for losses or to protect their herds. Wolves test our tolerance, compassion, ecological understanding, and wisdom. Will we as a society move forward or lurch backward in our policies toward them?

Predator Paranoia

"Lions and Tigers and Bears, oh my!" This unforgettable refrain from The Wizard of Oz reflects the attitude that some still have toward wild predators. As children we were read a litany of scary stories about animals, such as "Little Red Riding Hood" and "The Three Little Pigs." Today the media has picked up where Grimm's Fairy Tales left off, providing alarmist coverage of human/animal encounters. While it is wise to respect wild animals and keep a safe distance from them, we have instead become unduly paranoid and intolerant of them.

Lately, in the Seattle area, we've heard about two school lockdowns due to a Black Bear roaming near the suburban Bothell campuses. The presence of coyotes in Seattle neighborhoods has caused widespread panic. When a cougar showed up in Seattle's Discovery Park several years ago, people were discouraged from even entering this huge, 534-acre park, our city's largest. Do the facts justify our extreme fear of these wild predators living in our midst? Emphatically, no!

In the past hundred years in Washington State, there have only been fifteen cougar/human assaults and one fatality; there have been five bear assaults and one fatality. According to wolf experts, Jim and Jamie Dutcher, only two human fatalities have been caused by wolves in a hundred years in the entire U.S.

According to a Washington Department of Wildlife "Living with Wildlife Fact Sheet" (boldface emphasis is mine), **There were no documented coyote attacks on humans in Washington state until 2006**. In April 2006, Washington Department of Fish and Wildlife officers euthanized two coyotes in Bellevue (King County) after two young children were bitten while their parents were nearby. Coyotes had also scratched and snapped at two women and charged a man in the same area. These coyotes' unusually aggressive behavior likely resulted from being fed by people."

So how do these exceedingly rare attacks from wildlife compare to numbers of attacks from other people and their pet dogs?

In King County, Washington there were 450 attacks on humans by pet dogs in 2009; in Seattle there were 1,973 assaults and 19 homicides in 2010; the State of Washington had 20,599 violent offenses in 2010 and 154 murders.

Who are you afraid of now? I will take my chances with cougars, bears, and coyotes.

Chapter 7 - The Joy of Birding

What's In Your Back Yard?

Woody birding in his back yard
© Lori Cohen

One of the greatest free pleasures is counting birds in your back yard or neighborhood park. It requires no travel and is therapeutic. This is a fine way to start the day and only takes twenty minutes.

Here's how it works: go outside, preferably in the early morning. Dress for the weather and bring four things: a cup of coffee, binoculars, a note pad, and a pencil. You might want to add a bird identification book to this list. Then sit quietly for twenty minutes.

Watch, listen, and take notes. Look at the sky as well as the trees, buildings, and the landscape around you. Don't do anything else; this is not the time to multitask. It almost does not matter if you see birds or wildlife, because the calming effect of the watching is so beneficial. If you are quiet and patient you will experience a lot. In addition to the various birds, squirrels, raccoons, opossum, cats, and dogs you may see, you will notice the sounds, activities, smells, wind, weather, and clouds of your neighborhood.

A raccoon once stood and stared at me for five seconds while I admonished him for even thinking about eating our garden vegetables. A House Finch landed and perched on our deck railing three feet away. Anna's and Rufous Hummingbirds have buzzed by me at close range. A Sharp-Shinned Hawk once silenced the yard with its presence, then sat and watched me for nearly the entire twenty minutes I was there. Once, an escaped pet Cockatoo flew down our alley.

Yes, you will also hear sirens, garbage trucks, traffic, car alarms, train whistles, mechanical tools, and other urban noise. But even in the city these sounds abate at times—besides, they are part of our neighborhood soundscape.

In an era when so many are distracted, wired, on the phone, online, on mobile devices, or mentally somewhere else, this is your chance to tune in: to actually *be here now*. What do you see and hear? I see fifty-plus species of birds each year in my north Seattle back yard, ranging from finches to raptors. In spring, the bird song is fabulous. It is the best time of year to practice birding by ear. Oftentimes, ideas flow into your head; you take notice of simple pleasures such as a spring breeze, a cloud formation, a sunrise, or the distant (in my case) smell of Puget Sound. If you count birds, log your sightings into ebird. org. In so doing, you can participate in meaningful data gathering and be part of citizen science. The main point, though, is to go outside, be quiet, look up, and listen. You will be rewarded.

Birding Can (Should) Be Fun

"It's just a (common) bird," or worse yet a "It's a junk bird…." or "It's a trash bird…." Ever heard these irreverent remarks? They are typically made by serious birders when they spot something common or non-native. These birders are so jaded that they fail to appreciate that they are in glorious places watching beautiful, athletic birds. They're simply out to find the next "new" species for their birding life lists.

All birds are special, miraculous creatures, so why not show some respect for them? In addition, shouldn't we be encouraging other people to get excited when they see birds—all types of birds—so that they become interested in them and in preserving their habitat?

This raises an important issue in the world of birding, and one that does not get talked about often: snobbery. Some birders, bird organizations, and even birding tours, have found ways to be elitist, exclusive, and snobbish. This is bad for birding, bad for the birds themselves, and for conservation. We need more, not fewer, people to care about birds, and we need a whole lot more people to care about conservation.

People often ask me when I'm out birding if I've seen any "good" birds lately. When I reply that all birds are good, they usually scowl or harrumph and then move on. Others demean birds by calling them "junk birds, trash birds," or even "Euro-trash." The latter moniker is ironic, because it could also refer to millions of human beings in North America including me. And then there are the snooty birders who only care about rarities. For them, marveling at or learning about the behavior of something like an American Robin or a Dark-eyed Junco is a waste of time. Their cup is always more than half empty, since rarities are—as the name implies—hard to find. It's a hell of a way to live life, being disappointed most of the time.

Thankfully, not all birders are like this. Instead, many of us are appreciative, joyful, excited, and even have a sense of humor while we're birding. After all, these creatures are flying miracles that exhibit beauty and amazing behavior on a daily basis. Many migrate from far-away places. They sing incredible songs; they eat prey ranging from seeds and fruits, to worms, fish, small mammals, and copious quantities of bugs. Birds enrich our lives in countless ways. They inspire us. Shouldn't we revere them? I think so.

Birding for Under $100

A friend of mine recently became hooked on birding. She started without binoculars or field guides, nothing except for her camera and keen eyes (she is a professional photographer). My friend is living proof that birding need not be a costly pastime. Yes, there are high-end optics and all manner of gear that can cost thousands. But for those who want to get started and enjoy this wonderful hobby, you can do so for a hundred dollars or less. Just ask Roniq Bartanen: "I found a nice 8X42 pair of Nikon Trailblazer binoculars at Eagle Optics www.eagleoptics.com/binoculars for ninety dollars. Then I bought *Forest and Rangeland Birds of the United States*, a Forest Service Agriculture Handbook at a used bookstore for only three dollars. I'm really enjoying birding in my back yard in Seattle, in local refuges, and when I visit my dad in Texas. This inexpensive starter kit has opened up a whole new world to me."

Inspired by her early success, she continued bargain shopping at used book stores for birding resource guides, "I hit up Half Price Books over the weekend and found an awesome book titled *An Audubon Handbook: How to Identify Birds* used, for $6.49, as well as one of those cool laminated pocket naturalist folding guides to Washington birds for $2.99. I saw a copy of *Kingbird Highway* as well, but had reached my buying limit for that night and thought I'd get it from the library instead."

Kenn Kaufman's classic book *Kingbird Highway* chronicles his big year of birding when he was a young man equipped with an inexpensive pair of binoculars, a back pack, basic camping gear, and his thumb for hitch-hiking. He has since become one of the nation's premier birders.

Another birding classic, *The Big Year*, further demonstrates that this avocation can be pursued inexpensively. The *Big Year* book and film, both based on a true story, showcase one of the three "contestants" who competed to see who could identify the most birds in a year. This contestant quit his job at a nuclear plant, and lived in his car surviving on peanut butter sandwiches to fulfill his dream of having a big year of birding. I started with opera glasses and a Golden field guide to birds. It's not about the gear; it's about the experience.

Snipe Hunting

Wilson's Snipe
© Jeff Larsen

Remember the goofy Snipe Hunts that some of us engaged in at summer camp? Often they took place at night and involved a large sack, a club, and a flashlight. They were never successful, and those who went on them were considered gullible.

Sometimes, I think birders are on a lifelong Snipe Hunt, searching for elusive avifauna in difficult-to-access wild places. The search for the Ivory-Billed Woodpecker comes to mind—a bird species that has not been seen for years, and many believe has become extinct. But here's the good news: Snipe hunts actually *can* be successful—especially when you go during the day time, lose the bags, clubs, and flashlights, and instead visit a marsh or moist field with a good pair of binoculars.

On a recent tour of Ridgefield National Wildlife Refuge in southwestern Washington, we saw four Wilson's Snipe. These remarkable shore birds are stocky in stature with an oversized bill and distinctive head stripes. They are common across North America in wet grassy areas. In some ways, they are a good subject for an impossible hunt, because they are so well camouflaged that they blend in with their dense wetland surroundings.

Wilson's Snipe find and feed on invertebrates in the mud, using their long bill to find insect larvae, worms, crustaceans, and mollusks. They nest on the ground, and their thatched nests are often near water.

During breeding season, Wilson's Snipe make a haunting, wavering, sound reminiscent of owl tones in a fluttering cadence often heard at dawn and dusk. This sound helps them establish territory and attract potential mates. It is made by the wind whistling past their outstretched tail feathers after they first fly up and then descend rapidly. I will never forget hearing this haunting sound repeatedly at Malheur National Wildlife Refuge in southeastern Oregon, another great place for Snipe hunting. Just say, yes, when you have the opportunity to go on the next Snipe hunt—for the real ones that is.

Halloween Icon

Barred Owl
© Woody Wheeler

Some birding spots are so good that you anticipate a surprise bird encounter whenever you visit them. Union Bay Natural Area (UBNA) in Seattle is one such place. Earlier this week, while leading a tour there for a couple from Texas, we had a big surprise: the first Barred Owl ever seen at UBNA! It took me fifteen years and one-hundred-plus visits to UBNA to see an owl of any kind here. Connie Sidles, author of *In My Nature* and *Second Nature*, books about exploring the wilds of UBNA, *aka* Montlake Fill, confirmed that this was indeed the first Barred Owl sighting at the Fill. When I took her to see it shortly after our first owl encounter she was overcome with emotion.

Actually, a flock of Bushtits saw it first. They buzzed and chattered in such an agitated manner that I was alerted to the presence of a predator. Just around the corner, I found the Barred Owl perched twelve feet up in an alder tree. Three Anna's Hummingbirds hovered a few feet away, seemingly about to spear the owl with their thin, sharp bills. This owl had caused quite a commotion.

Barred Owls are relatively large owls of the moist woodlands. They hunt mostly by sound, primarily at night. During day they conceal themselves in dense vegetation and tree cavities. Barred Owls eat small mammals, amphibians, reptiles, and invertebrates. They nest in tree cavities or in abandoned open nests made by crows or hawks.

In the last few decades, Barred Owls have expanded their range westward from their former range in the eastern United States, bridging across northern Canada, all the way to the State of Washington. They were first seen in eastern Washington in 1965 and are now found in most forested areas of the state.

Another species of owl probably wishes the Barred Owl had not expanded its range westward: the closely related Northern Spotted Owl, currently listed as Threatened on the U.S. Endangered Species list. Although they do not require old-growth forests to live and reproduce as do Northern Spotted

Owls, Barred Owls will penetrate these forests in search of food and habitat, and they can and will kill and displace Spotted Owls.

During spring and summer you might hear Barred Owls' distinctive hoot with a southern accent: "Who cooks for you-all." Most populations of Barred Owls are increasing, and this one sighted in UBNA is yet another example of their increasing range.

Magical sightings like this happen when you have your head up and your senses engaged. You don't have to go to Costa Rica (although I highly recommend it) to see natural wonders. When you do go out to the local woods tonight, you never know WHO you might find.

Hanging Out With Mixed Flocks

Winter birding can be slow at times. Then all at once, a cloud of different bird species appears. Noisy social and alarm calls signal their arrival, at times punctuated by the beat of a woodpecker. If you hold still and are quiet, the flock will move right past you. You will become immersed in a mixed flock!

In western Washington, you might first notice the Kinglets. Golden-crowned Kinglets come down to eye-level, so you can see them much more easily and with far less neck strain than when they are high in the canopy of conifer trees. Ruby-crowned Kinglets are the boldest. They perch within a few feet of you, and sometimes raise their ruby crown as they chatter away in Morse code-like phrases. Accompanying the Kinglets are often Black-capped and Chestnut-backed Chickadees, Dark-eyed Juncos, Bushtits, Spotted Towhees, Steller's Jays, Red-breasted Nuthatches, Yellow-rumped Warblers, the occasional Anna's Hummingbird, Bewick's Wren, Brown Creeper, and Downy Woodpecker. Other species might join in too. It's an impressive assembly, all in constant motion.

What makes birds, usually known for their territoriality, hang out together in mixed flocks? Two main factors seem to be at play. First, mixed flocking behavior occurs primarily in the non-breeding season when they are far less territorial. Second, it occurs when food is scarce, usually in the winter. By flocking together, birds benefit from group feeding opportunities and the built-in alarm system that a large number of birds provides. Birds in mixed flocks can spend more time feeding and less time watching for predators. By joining a mixed flock, they will also find more food by noticing where and how other birds forage.

As David Sibley said in *The Sibley Guide to Bird Life and Behavior*, "Flocking is also partially a response to the problem of searching for food, as many eyes can search a large region more effectively than a single pair of eyes." Finally, mixed flocks may confuse predators as members of the flock flee in multiple directions. Be patient and observant on your next winter walk in a woodland or park. Eventually, you will see a flutter of activity or hear a lively chorus of bird calls. When you do, pause, be quiet, and look up: you might have just encountered a mixed flock of birds.

Reuniting With Ptarmigan

Last week, on the flanks of Mount Rainier, I had my first encounter with White-Tailed Ptarmigan in decades. First I heard soft clucking, then after scanning distant slopes without spotting a single bird, I found them practically at my feet. An adult stood sentry while two chicks moved slowly about the rocks, squeezing into crevices to become even more camouflaged than they already were.

Few creatures can survive in the alpine tundra. White-tailed Ptarmigan, the smallest species of North American grouse, can. Breeding American Pipits and Gray-crowned Rosy Finches spend part of the year here. Pikas, Marmots, Mountain Goats, Golden-mantled Ground Squirrels, and Least Chipmunks also inhabit this scenic but climatically tough neighborhood.

White-tailed Ptarmigan are uniquely adapted to living in this cold, harsh environment. They have feathered toes, cryptic plumage, and an energy-conserving lifestyle that involves little unnecessary movement. Their feet have been referred to as "avian snowshoes." During winter, they develop dense feathering on both sides of their feet and their claws become longer. These adaptations provide insulation, a firm platform on soft snow and good traction. Their beautiful plumage morphs from brown, patterned tones in the summer to all white in the winter so that they match their surroundings.

White-tailed Ptarmigan nest in shallow depressions that they line with fine grass, lichens, leaves, and flowers. Their diet consists of some of the same things: buds, stems, seeds, leaves, flowers, and insects.

Like another high-elevation specialist, the American Pika, White-tailed Ptarmigan are stressed by warmer temperatures. They will often bathe in the snow when temperatures exceed 70 degrees Fahrenheit. Unlike Pikas, their population is apparently not at risk, at least for now. According to The International Union for Conservation of Nature and Natural Resources, White-tailed Ptarmigan is a species of "Least Concern."

It is always a treat to encounter these exquisitely patterned birds and often a surprise. Due to their superb camouflage and quiet, sedentary nature, they can be nearly under your feet without gaining your notice. I recall having a boisterous lunch years ago with friends in the North Cascades and noticing White-tailed Ptarmigan only after they moved slightly when we stood up to leave. We had been sitting, literally, beside them for thirty minutes. They stand still, calmly watching you with their reddish eyes, perhaps knowing that you will not be staying long in their world of the alpine tundra.

Floating Art

If you appreciate art, that is reason enough to watch birds. Each year, wintering ducks are on display throughout North America, dressed in their finest plumages.

Art Exhibit A: Wood Duck

Wood Duck
© Larry Hubbell

Would it be possible to design more beautiful creatures? On the verge of extinction in the early 1900s, Wood Ducks have since not only recovered, but have expanded their range. This was due to an enlightened combination of hunting restrictions, the placement of numerous artificial nest boxes, and wetland preservation. Bellrose in 1976, cited in Cornell Lab of Ornithology's *Handbook of Bird Biology*, referred to it as "one of the most complete population recoveries ever witnessed in North America."

Art Exhibit B: Gadwall

Yes, Wood Ducks are stunning, but so are Gadwalls. Note the exquisite pattern on the breast of the Gadwall pictured on the next page. This beautiful, intricate pattern resembles tweed or herringbone patterns on human clothing.

According to Ducks Unlimited, some half million ducks spend their winter on Puget Sound, including North American Wigeon, Pintail, Green-winged Teal, Goldeneye (both kinds), Bufflehead, Long-tailed Duck, Scoter (three kinds), as well as year-round residents such as Mallard and Gadwall. These ducks are dressed in their finest attire. Why? Because they seek new mates each winter, and their beautiful plumage helps distinguish them from numerous species that inhabit these waters together.

This incredible display of vivid colors and striking patterns can help lift the gloom of winter days. Go see it at a lake, pond, river, or shoreline near you. You won't regret it. It is one of the finest art exhibits on the planet. All you have to do is to look up.

Gadwall
© Woody Wheeler

Epilogue

Many of us have lost touch with nature. As we sit indoors for hours in front of electronic screens, we become disconnected from everything that the outdoor world has to offer.

Imagine if you went through life without discovering art or music. Now imagine going through life without ever noticing birds, other wildlife, trees, plants, the ever-changing sky-scape, and a myriad of other natural wonders here on earth. Consider that there are over 900 species of birds and 210 species of mammals in North America alone, not to mention countless smaller organisms. Those who are wired into the zombie-mode or trapped in a human-centric existence often fail to notice that these other inhabitants of our planet even exist. It does not matter who you are or where you live, nature in some form is available to all of us, in parks, in back yards, on balconies, out windows, and in the sky. Just by noticing it, we can experience the simple—even inspiring—pleasures that exist all around us.

Tuning in to natural phenomena can enrich our lives and our appreciation for the incredible planet that we inhabit. We stand to benefit in more ways than we know by doing so, and so does the earth. In the words of the great naturalist and writer Robert Michael Pyle: "People who care, conserve; people who don't know, don't care."

Looking up is the first step toward appreciating our natural world, which is vital to its conservation. My hope is that you take this first step and that you find it to your liking.

Glossary

Biodiversity	The great variety of living organisms on earth.
Conservation	The wise and prudent use of natural resources.
Deforestation	Removing the forest cover and converting it into a developed landscape.
Ecology	The study of the relationships between living things and their environment.
Ecosystem	The living and non-living components of a particular area, and the ecological processes that bind them together.
Ephemeral	Short-lived, such as a plant with a brief life cycle.
Equinox	The time twice a year when the sun crosses the celestial equator, usually around March 20 and September 22.
Extirpated	When a species is removed from a part of its range.
Glacial Erratic	Large rocks that were carried and deposited by glaciers.
Invertebrate	Any animal without a backbone, such as insects, spiders, crustaceans, worms, and mollusks (squids, snails, shrimp, and clams).
Irruption	Irregular migratory movements that depend upon factors such as food and territory availability and/or a change in seasons.
Mixed flock	When birds of different species flock together—usually during non-breeding seasons—to enhance food resources and safety.
Monoculture	A landscape dramatically simplified to cultivate primarily one crop, such as lawns, agricultural crop lands, or tree farms.

Niche	The role played by a species in its particular environment.
Onomatopoetic	A voice imitating a natural sound.
Ornithology	The study of birds.
Pheromone	Chemical substances secreted by animals, which convey information to and produce responses in individuals of the same species.
Philopatry	Site fidelity shown by species that return to the exact same breeding grounds and to specific points along the way on their migrations.
Riparian	Waterside vegetation alongside oceans, lakes, rivers, creeks, and other bodies of water. Riparian zones are rich in biodiversity.
Solstice	The two times of year when the sun reaches its furthest northern and southern distance from the celestial equator, on December 21 (Winter Solstice in Northern Hemisphere) and June 21 (Summer Solstice in Northern Hemisphere).
Sexually Dimorphic	When males and females of the same species have distinctly different appearances and/or size.
Torpor	A profound state of sleep in which the body temperature drops and metabolic processes and stimulus-reaction processes slow down. Birds may enter torpor on a nightly or an extended period during cold weather.

Bibliography

Books

Alison, Mark, editor. *City Birding, True Tales of Birds and Birdwatching in Unexpected Places.* Stackpole Books Publishing, 2003.

Bell, Brian and Kennedy, Gregory. *Birds of Washington State.* Lone Pine Publishing, 2006.

Cain, Susan. *Quiet.* Broadway Paperbacks, 2012.

Carson, Robert J., editor. *Where the Great River Bends—A Natural and Human History of the Columbia at Wallula.* Keokee Co. Publishing, Inc., 2008.

Cornell Lab of Ornithology. *Handbook of Bird Biology.* Princeton University Press, 2004.

Darwin, Charles. *Voyage of the Beagle.* Beagle Press, 1839.

De La Pena, Martin and Rumboll, Maurice. *Birds of Southern South America.* Princeton University Press, 1998.

Dietrich, William. *Green Fire: A History of Huxley College.* Huxley College of the Environment Publisher, 2011.

Dunn, Jon L. and Alderfer, Jonathan. *National Geographic Field Guide to the Birds of North America—6th Edition.* National Geographic Publications, 2012.

Dutcher, Jim. *Living with Wolves.* Mountaineers Books, 2008

Egan, Timothy. *The Big Burn.* Mariner Books publishing, 2009.

Ehrlich, Paul R., Dobkin, David S., Wheye, Darryl. *The Birder's Handbook: A Field Guide to The Natural History of North American Birds.* Simon & Schuster publications, 1988.

Geisel, Theodore. *The Lorax.* Random House Publishing, 1971.

Gill, Frank B. *Ornithology.* W.H. Freeman and Company publication, 1990.

Grese, Robert E. Jens Jensen, *Maker of Natural Parks and Gardens.* The Johns Hopkins University Press, 1992.

Guralnik, David B, Editor in Chief. *Webster's New World Dictionary.* Simon and Schuster publishing, 1980.

Jensen, Jens. *Siftings.* Ralph Fletcher Seymour publishing, 1939.

Kaufman, Kenn. *Birds of North America.* Houghton Mifflin Harcourt Publishing, 2001.

Kaufman, Lynn Hassler. *Hummingbirds of the American West.* Rio Nuevo Publishers, 2002.

Kittredge, William. *Hole in the Sky.* Random House Publishing, 1992.

Larson, Erik. *Devil in the White City.* Vintage Publishing, 2004.

Link, Russell. *Landscaping for Wildlife in the Pacific Northwest.* University of Washington Press, 1999.

Lonely Planet Series 8th Edition: *Argentina.* Lonely Planet Publications, 2012.

Morris, Edmund. *Theodore Rex, Biography of Teddy Roosevelt.* Random House Publishing, 2002.

Niemeyer, Carter. *Wolfer.* Bottlefly Press, 2012.

Northcutt, Wendy. *The Darwin Awards: Evolution in Action.* Dutton publishers, 2000.

Obmascik, Mark. *The Big Year.* Altra Books publications, 2011.

Sibley, David Allen. *The Sibley Guide to Birds.* David Allen Sibley: Alfred Knopf Publications, 2000.

Sibley, David Allen. *The Sibley Guide to Bird Life & Behavior.* Alfred Knopf Publications, 2001.

Sniderman-Bachrach, Julia. *The City in a Garden: A Photographic History of Chicago's Parks.* The Center for American Places Publications, 2001.

Stokes, Donald and Lillian. *Stokes Field Guide to Birds of North America.* Little Brown and Company, 2010.

Rosenthal, Norman. *Winter Blues*. Guilford Press, 2013.

Williams, Terry Tempest. *Refuge*. Pantheon Books, 1991.

Wuerthner, George. *Yellowstone: a Visitor's Companion*. Stackpole Books, 1992.

Articles/Other Publications

"A Fierce Advocate for Grizzlies Sees Warning Signs for the Bear." *Yale Environment 360 , 2010*

Brown, Matthew. "Whitebark Pines Ailing, but Don't Get Protections." *Seattle Times*, July 18, 2012

Clark, Patterson. "Birds of Different Feathers Flock Together." Urban Jungle Feature, *Washington Post*, Feb. 1, 2011.

French, Brett. "Northern Park Elk Population Still Dropping." *Billings Gazette,* March 8, 2013

Goldman, Jason G. "Are All Home Gardens the Same?" *Conservation Weekly Dispatch*, a University of Washington publication, March 19, 2014

Gore, Al. "Climate of Denial." *Rolling Stone*, June 22, 2011

Gorgi, Uki. "The Ugly American Environmentalist." *Time World*, March 1, 2007

Harris, Van. "Vultures are Scary but Beneficial to Environment." *Memphis Commercial Appeal* October 26, 2012

Leonard, Pat. "A Season of Snowy Owls." *Living Bird*, Cornell Lab of Ornithology, Spring 2014

Lynch, Kathy. "Yellowstone Still the Best Place for Watching Wolves despite Many Killed in Hunt." T*he Wildlife News*, July 13, 2013. www.thewildlifenews.com/2013/07/09/ kathie-lynch-july-9-2013

Ostrom, Carol. "Dangerous Distraction." *The Seattle Times* December 13, 2012

Platt, John, "The Great Sparrow Campaign Was the Start of the Greatest Mass Starvation in History." *Mother*

Nature News Network.
www.mnn.com/earth-matters/animals/stories

Reis, Patrick. "American Pika Denied Endangered Species Status." *Scientific American*, February 5, 2010

Ricks, Delthia. "Study: Texting while driving now leading cause of death for teen drivers." *Newsday.com* May 8, 2013

Romano, Andrew. "How Dumb Are We?" *Newsweek Magazine*, March 28, 2011.

Sager, Kim. "Whitebark Pine Seeds, Red Squirrels, and Grizzly Bears: An Interconnected Relationship." *University of Idaho*, 2009

"Surnames Can Determine Buying Behavior." *United Press International*, Business Section. January 23, 2011

Conniff, Richard. "The Evil of the Outdoor Cat." *New York Times*, March 23, 2014

Wang, Karissa S. *"Turn Ballard Green, Plant a Tree." Seattle Times*, April 17, 2012

Welch, David and Armstrong, Joshua. "GM's Cruze Drawing Prius Owners Powers Small-Car Revival." *Bloomberg Business and Financial News*, August 15, 2011

"Whitebark Pine." *Grand Teton Resource Brief*, 2011

"Whitebark Pine in the Greater Yellowstone Ecosystem." *Greater Yellowstone Network Brief*, April 2012

"Wind Energy and Avian Protection" *Puget Sound Energy brochure*

Wind Energy Facts in Washington, 2012

Woodyard, Chris. "Vehicles Keep Inching Up and Putting on Pounds." *USA Today*, July 15, 2007

Websites

All About Birds, Cornell Lab of Ornithology website:
www.allaboutbirds.com

Arctic Studies Center website:

www. www.naturalhistory.si.edu/arctic/

Center for Biological Diversity: Howling for Justice (wolf blog): *howlingforjustice.wordpress.com*

Deep Root, Green Infrastructure for Your Community April 2010 *"Tree Cover %—How Does Your City Measure Up?": www.deeproot.com*

Green Cities Alliance Tree Report, Sept 2012: www.forterra.org/press_releases/seattletreereport

Defenders of Wildlife website: www.defenders.org

Denmark Points Way in Alternative Energy Resources: topics. nytimes.com/top/news/business/energy-environment/wind-power/index.html

Ducks Unlimited: www.ducks.org

Friends of North Creek Forest, Bothell, Washington: www.friendsofnorthcreekforest.com

George C. Reifel Migratory Bird Sanctuary in Delta, British Columbia, Canada: www.reifelbirdsanctuary.com

Greater Yellowstone Coalition website: www.greateryellowstone.org

"How Denmark Sees the World in 2012." Time Science : content.time.com/time/health/article/0,8599,1828874,00.html

Iberá Project website: www.proyectoibara.org; www.Tompkinsconservation. org

Idaho State website: www.idaho.gov

Montana State Website: www.mt.gov

Seattle Police Department Crime Statistics: www.seattle.gov/police/crime/stats.htm

Seattle Urban Forest Management Plan; Seattle reLeaf website:
    www.seattle.gov/trees
The Conservation Land Trust website:
    www.conservationlandtrust.org
Vestas Wind Energy Company, Denmark:
    www.vestas.com
U.S. Fish and Wildlife Service; Wind Power News, New York
    Times June 2012:
    www.awea.org
Washington Department of Wildlife Living with Wildlife
    website:
    wdfw.wa.gov/living
Washington Association of Sheriffs and Police Chiefs:
    www.icrimewatch.net/washington.php
Wyoming State website:
    www.wyoming.gov

Applications
I-Bird Pro birding app

Film/ DVD
Lundin, Carey. *Jens Jensen, The Living Green*. Viva Lundin
Productions, 2013

Author Biography

Woody Wheeler is a Master Birder, a Certified Interpretive Guide, and the owner of Conservation Catalyst, a birding and natural history firm. He previously worked for The Nature Conservancy, Audubon Society and Seattle Parks Foundation. Connecting people with nature is his passion, and he does this through trips, classes, presentations, and by writing nature blogs on his website (www.conservationcatalyst.com).

Wheeler leads tours for Naturalist Journeys, Seattle Parks, Audubon Washington, Seattle Parks Foundation, Friends of Burke Gilman Trail, Earth Corps and for private clients. Recent tours include: Big Bend National Park and the Davis Mountains, Grand Yellowstone; Montana Prairies; and Washington State's Olympic Peninsula and Cascade Loops.

Wheeler holds Environmental Studies and Geography degrees from Western Washington University. He studied Ornithology at the University of Washington and took the Master Birding Class at Seattle Audubon and the Cornell Lab of Ornithology Bird Biology Class. He believes that learning about nature should be engaging, inclusive and joyful.

If you want to get on the path to be a published author by Influence Publishing please go to www.InfluencePublishing.com

Inspiring books that influence change

More information on our other titles and how to submit your own proposal can be found at www.InfluencePublishing.com